The final usefulness of my Catholic training was to teach me, together with much that proved to be practical, a conception of something prior to and beyond utility ("Consider the lilies of the field; they toil not, neither do they spin"), an idea of sheer wastefulness that is always shocking to non-Catholics . . .

Mary McCarthy

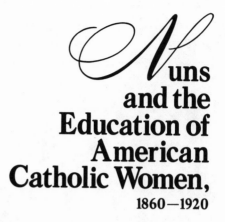

Nuns and the Education of American Catholic Women, 1860–1920

Eileen Mary Brewer

 LOYOLA UNIVERSITY PRESS

Loyola University Press
3441 North Ashland Avenue
Chicago, IL 60657

Library of Congress Cataloging-in-Publication Data

Brewer, Eileen Mary, 1952-
  Nuns and the education of American Catholic
women, 1860-1920.
    Bibliography: p. 197
    1. Women—Education (Secondary)—United States—
History.   2. Catholic schools—United States—History.
3. Convents and nunneries—United States—History.
I. Title.
LC1755.B74   1987   376'.5'0973   87-3544
ISBN 0-8294-0571-2

Designed by C. L. Tornatore

To my parents
Mary O'Brien Brewer
and
Thomas Martin Brewer

Contents

Foreword

To say that this is *(a)* a book about nuns and high school girls and *(b)* an important and lively contribution to American social history may seem to be a contradiction in terms to many potential readers. Such a readership may be divided three ways. First, a tiny but important third is nostalgic about the lost world of the old style parochial school. Members of this group provide clienteles for books and plays like the one called *Do Black Patent Leather Shoes Really Reflect Up?* Their less good natured counterparts look back on the nuns and students of this lost world as participants in a privileged world forever lost because of changes resulting from the Second Vatican Council and vandals who misinterpret the tendencies of that Council.

A second tiny third engages in enduring rage against that world of nuns and high school students. Eileen Brewer includes a couple of early examples of this type, the great essayist Agnes Repplier and the novelist Kate Chopin who got grist for their writings or substance for their memoirs by kicking their adult black patent leather shoes at the nuns they remember, at the school walls that they saw as imprisoning. Today only a dwindling senior generation could be in this camp, and one must surmise that some ex-Catholics or ex-parochial school students who never went to such schools keep inventing them in their minds so they have someone around to kick, someone on whom to shift blame for what goes wrong in their adult lives.

The third potential cohort of readers is by far the largest. It is made up of Americans, Catholic, Protestant, Jewish, and Apathetic, who do not know about the world of Catholic academies at the turn of the century, and who may not care. While the nostalgic and the rejective can easily be tantalized into this book in order to check out their memories and impressions and do some comparing, the larger part of the population has to be lured on other grounds.

I find at least two of these, right from the beginning. First, the story is well told. I watched it develop during the period of Eileen Brewer's research, observed her struggle with the problem of lost sources or puzzles in surviving ones. From those efforts came drafts of chapters that struck me as revealing a good narrative line, a sense of the significant detail and the substantial main theme, an ability to hold the reader. Rereading this book after several years confirms that impression. As she deftly and swiftly moves from brief stops in medieval Europe, in the founding of modern religious orders, and the establishing of schools, she quickly proceeds to discuss four orders of women and their schools.

Her slice of history cuts mainly through the American Midwest, and there could be subtle differences had she chosen to deal with Canada or the American Northeast or wherever else. Yet, every history has to be about somewhere and some time, and good historians help enlarge if not universalize their stories not by painting with broad strokes on huge billboards but by being attentive to the profoundly human dimensions of what is in front of them. Thus many of us who are not Hasidic Jews or Japanese have found ourselves engaged by books that concentrate on such worlds and help make them our own. You do not have to have "been there" to become a part of this story. Almost no one alive could have "been there," since this story stops in 1920. Yet in the mind's eye, one will be drawn there.

The second reason has to do with the book not as a literary object but as a contribution to social history. It helps explain not only the world we have lost but the world we inhabit. America is made up of many kinds of peoples, with differing kinds of memories. There is no generic American plot. Would this have been a "typical" story had Brewer chosen to deal with the sons of Boston Brahmins, who in their time wielded power of a sort these Catholics could not have dreamed to hold? Would this be "everyone's book" right off, had she concentrated on the children of midwestern Protestant small towners? Those who cherish *Tom Sawyer* and Norman Rockwell might think so.

The America we inherit, however, is not just that of Boston Brahmins, Iowa Protestants, or anyone else, for that matter. The parents and kin of these nuns and their charges arrived from Europe in such numbers and "arrived" in the American social order so rapidly that soon it was they who were running the cities, waiting for their turn in American political and intellectual life. No one can tell the American story whole without concentrating on parts. Here is a significant one.

If I have one quibble with the plot, and all reviewers and Foreword writers should assert their independence or display their credentials by doing some quibbling, it is this: Brewer speaks of this parochial world—and it was parochial—as a ghetto, which in a way it was. Yet there is a tinge or at least a tingelet of envy for those outside such a ghetto, a hint of resentment at the guardians of its gates, a suggestion that a large world could have or should have been available to these young women. Yes and no. I have argued elsewhere that, yes, there was a Catholic ghetto back then. But it was not sequestered from a world of pluralist interaction but was instead a ghetto among all the other ghettos. The children of the Adamses and the Jameses of New York in expatriation in Europe inhabited large worlds. Yet they were intricate, sheltered, bound by their own prejudices and shortsightednesses. These days we have to visit any number of these sheltered worlds in order to learn about the America we inherited. In fact, despite intermarriage, rage against old or-

ders, social mobility, suburbanization, mass higher education, mass media, or whatever, most Americans still live in
parochial and provincial subsectors of the social economy.
They do, at least, if they are fortunate. They may later have
identity crises, but they belong to something strong enough
to have given them an identity in the first place.

There are some side benefits as well. For example, one
here learns how much American Catholicism in particular
and American religion in general involve not dogma so much
as behavior. These schools, grimly preoccupied as their
teachers may have been by the truths of Catholic faith and
the truths about life, existed chiefly to habituate their students in a way of life, to make certain behavior patterns
reflexive. This is a case study that reveals much about that
dimension of American nurture.

Second, the story inspires reflection on nurture. At
times Dr. Brewer at least implicitly scores the nuns for resisting social causes like woman suffrage. The modern reader,
however, has to know that they were not alone. Down the
street in those decades were progressive Protestant Social
Gospel leaders who almost unanimously resisted woman
suffrage. They were out to protect what today we call the
Victorian family and model of womanhood. Both camps may
have been wrong; they were wrong about some things. Yet
they saw forces they could not understand tearing at social
fabric that had some values they wanted to cherish. It would
be unfair to think that these nuns alone kept their students
away from exposure to such forces of change.

Third, Brewer helps recreate the world of motivations
among the sisters who ran and taught in the academies. This
book might have been much different had a Freudian or
Marxist reductionist written it, someone who was sure that
these women were "nothing but" this or that. Brewer grasps
what moderns often forget: that both what was good and
what was bad about their social world was a true belief that
they were spreading and helped assure Christian salvation.
That heaven and hell represented stark alternatives. That the
life to come was very real and, through devotion and practice, already partly accessible. That they were called by God

and that they had taken vows to contribute to the scheme of salvation. And they successfully imparted something of this drama to the girls who joined the religious orders, those who became Catholic homemakers, and even the non-Catholics who were there not to be proselytized but who evidently found something of that drama to be plausible and not wholly unattractive.

There are dark, gray passages and corridors in these schools and in this plot. Brewer lightens some of them by talking about "accomplishments" and "mischiefs," about the not always welcome individualism of the children. She does so without making their world seem merely quaint, bizarre, or arcane. This is anything but bold propaganda for the world of the Catholic academy back then. It is a subtle program of attentiveness to the real lives of real people who make up parts of what we call the real world. It beckons readers to observe that program in order to inform the plots of their own, probably very, very different lives.

Martin E. Marty
The University of Chicago

Acknowledgments

*J*oseph M. Curran deserves my first thanks for imparting to me both a respect and fascination for the complexity of human experience. I am also grateful to my graduate school adviser Martin E. Marty, whose openness and enthusiasm gave me the freedom and encouragement to pursue non-traditional ways of exploring the past. Special thanks are also due to Jerald C. Brauer, Emmet Larkin, and Lawrence J. McCaffrey for their provocative insights and stimulating conversation.

This book could not have been written without the cooperation and help of the religious orders whose schools I studied. I am deeply grateful to the Society of the Sacred Heart in America, the Sisters of Mercy of Chicago, the Sinsinawa Dominicans and the Sisters of Charity of the Blessed Virgin Mary. Sister Jane Coogan, B.V.M. deserves special thanks for her encouragement, assistance and inspiration during each stage of this project. I cannot adequately thank her for all she has done. The archivists of the Society of the Sacred Heart in America, Sister Mary C. Wheeler, R.S.C.J., and Sister Marie Martinez, R.S.C.J., provided generous assistance and gracious hospitality while I worked in their archives. The Society of the Sacred Heart's excellent archives are a tribute to their talent and hard work. Naturally, I am fully responsible for the interpretation of all materials found in the archives of these four religious orders as well as any mistakes that may have been made.

I am very grateful to Ellen Skerrett who generously shared with me her work and insights on the Chicago Archdiocese, the Irish in America, and American Catholicism. She was instrumental in the completion of this book. I am also indebted to Lamar Riley Murphy and Jane Hunter for their incisive criticism of this work. Edmund Ballantyne, Michael Greene, Joseph McShane, S.J., Janet Summers, and Ann Taves provided intellectual and emotional support throughout my years at the University of Chicago. Ruth Borenstein, Miriam Conrad, Patrick Davish, and Julie Overbaugh helped me keep body and soul together during the past three years in Boston. Most of all, I owe thanks to Jane Blumenthal and Virginia Fraser for their invaluable contribution to my book as well as their extraordinary friendship, patience, and love.

Finally, I wish to thank my family, Mary O'Brien Brewer, Thomas Brewer, Ann Masterberti, Kathleen Maher Trepal, Michael Trepal, and Robert Maher, for their unfailing love, understanding, and laughter.

Introduction

$\mathcal{T}$his book examines the role played by nuns in the intellectual, emotional, and religious formation of American Catholic women in the period between 1860 and 1920. During these years the Catholic church in the United States grew at an astounding pace and established parishes, schools, hospitals, and orphanages throughout the country. Catholics used these institutions to set themselves apart from Protestant America and to create an identity as American Catholics. Most important in this quest for unity and particularity were the schools.

Within this period of institutionalization, many Catholic girls received their secondary education in convent academies. At a time when American Catholicism was predominantly an immigrant religion, these academies functioned as elite schools in which ethnic identification was ignored. Because they aimed to form American Catholic gentlewomen, they drew their greatest support from the emerging Catholic middle class. For the most part, convent academies existed outside the structure of American Catholic parishes and parish schools. Moreover, in organization and development, the academies sharply differed from the Catholic high schools for girls, which were only able to take hold well after 1900.

Roman Catholic communities of women religious staffed and administered these isolated, all-female academies. Sisters injected religion into every aspect of institutional life, from the subjects studied to the games the girls played. No goal rivalled that of saving their pupils' souls. For the nuns, educating for sanctity meant shaping the lives of their pupils according to the values and ideals of the convent.[1]

Until the early twentieth century, convent academies provided the only Catholic secondary education available to girls. They reached their peak of popularity at a time when an increasing portion of non-Catholic girls began attending public high schools instead of Protestant or secular private academies.[2] Non-Catholic girls in this period also began attending colleges, which offered women a higher education comparable to that found in the finest men's colleges. This crucial development in the education of women had little impact on the nuns who taught in the academies, because the sisters looked only to the Catholic Church and their own religious communities for guidance in educational matters. The schooling of Catholic girls thus forms a separate chapter in the history of women's education in America.

Scholarly neglect of the education of Catholic girls from 1860 to 1920 has left untold a significant part of the American Catholic story. Only by entering the hidden world of the convent school can the historian begin to understand Catholic women and their effect on the development of the Church in America. This study describes a typical convent education in this period by considering the Catholic church's tradition of educating girls in Europe and America, examining particular religious orders who administered convent schools in the United States, studying in detail the academic, social, and religious life of selected academies and analyzing the expectations of the convent school world.

Background   1

The Development of a Tradition

American Catholic nuns inherited the centuries-old Christian tradition of female education. From its earliest years the church allowed women to receive an education for religious reasons. St. Jerome (342–420), a Church Father, set the pattern for this education when he allowed his friend Laerta's daughter, Paula, to study reading, writing, Latin, Greek, scripture, and the Early Fathers, because she had pledged herself to virginity and to Jesus Christ.

> When Paula comes to be a little older and to increase like her Spouse in wisdom and stature and favor with God and man, let her go with her parents to the temple of her true Father, but let her not come out of the temple with them. Let them seek her upon the world's highway amid the crowds and the throng of their kinsfolk, and let them find her nowhere but in the shrine of the Scriptures, questioning the prophets and apostles on the meaning of that spiritual marriage to which she is vowed.[1]

Other churchmen followed Jerome's advice on educating women for religion. Caesarius of Arles, a sixth-century monk and bishop, demanded literacy of all applicants to the convent. In his monastery he required one nun to read aloud while the others worked, and he encouraged all to think continually about scripture. He also wanted the abbess to encourage reading and praying among the nuns instead of embroidery and needlework.[2] In the twelfth century, Peter Abelard, a well-known theologian, recommended a program of study for the nuns in his friend Heloise's abbey. They learned Latin, Greek, and Hebrew in order to correctly understand scripture. Between all the offices of the day, Abelard insisted that the literate nuns were to read and receive instruction, while the illiterate were to do the manual work.[3]

The instructions of Abelard and Caesarius of Arles reflected the development of a tradition of learning for female monastics in the Middle Ages. Differences occurred according to century, region and particular house, but on the whole, the monasteries provided a few women with opportunities for education, organization, and responsibility.[4] Many of the monasteries also educated girls. A medieval biography of two accomplished eighth-century nuns, Herlinda and Renilda of Eyck, insisted that girls were sent to the monastery for the study of "divine doctrines, human arts, religious studies, and sacred letters."[5] In the York and Lincoln dioceses of England, over two-thirds of the nunneries had schools between the end of the thirteenth century and the middle of the sixteenth century. The nuns could read, write, and sing the services of the church.[6] Although rudimentary, these schools were a significant aspect of medieval education and provided almost the only alternative to a household education for girls.[7] French nuns also possessed some education and by the late twelfth century their schools were widespread and popular.[8]

German monasteries produced very well-educated nuns in the Middle Ages. The most famous of these monasteries was the Abbey of Gandersheim in ninth and tenth-century Saxony where Hrowsitha, the brilliant poet and dramatist, received an education. Her work reflected knowledge of Virgil, Lucan, Horace, Ovid, and Terence. She composed religious legends in Latin verse, seven dramas in the style of Terence, a poem on Otto the Great and a history of her monastery.[9] In the late twelfth century two other German nuns, Hildegarde of Bingen and Elizabeth of Schonau, achieved international reputations as mystics. Hildegarde's accounts of her visions reflected her acquaintance with Latin, scripture, the liturgy, biblical exegesis, music and natural sciences. She incorporated much of the scientific knowledge and religious thought of their time in her descriptions of her visions.[10]

Throughout the Middle Ages, women like Hroswitha and Hildegarde resided in monasteries and passed on their learning to others. Many of those entrusted to their care remained in the monastery for life. During the Middle Ages, men also received their educations in monastic institutions. Beginning in the thirteenth century, however, they shunned the monastery in favor of the university, which offered preparation for careers in law, government, medicine, and the church. Because women were barred from universities and the professions, their education continued to be confined to the monastery. In the fourteenth century, a small number of Italian women outside the cloister tried to join men in the revival of knowledge, but they were quickly silenced. Trained by their fathers or by male tutors, these women knew languages, history, literature, moral philosophy, and poetry.[11] A few, such as Isotta Nogorala and Laura Certi, achieved a certain degree of fame, despite criticism that they harbored male intellects in female bodies. As women were excluded from universities and denied the pursuit of knowledge outside the monastic walls, these Italian scholars had little choice but to marry, enter convents, or retreat into self-imposed exile.[12]

Yet a few men in the Renaissance expressed dissatisfaction with a schooling that prepared women only for virginity and the cloister. The Spanish humanist Juan Luis Vives (1462–1540) was the most important of these critics. He bridged the gap between old medieval ideas on women and new ideas for education of both sexes. On the one hand, Vives retained the medieval admiration for the nun as the ideal woman, emphasizing the conventual practices of silence, seclusion, piety, purity, and obedience for all women, whether single, married, widowed or cloistered.[13] On the other hand, he designed an educational program that would prepare women for the domestic duties of married life. Other humanists, such as the celebrated Erasmus (1469–1536), echoed Vives' cry for better-educated women and demanded a new standard of training for marriage and motherhood. Vives and those of similar mind aimed to form devout, moral ladies, affectionate wives and mothers, intellectual companions, and skilled mistresses of the home.[14]

The Ursulines, a group of teaching sisters founded in 1534 by Angela Merici, appropriated many of Vives' ideas. Like the Spanish humanist, this Italian sister believed in training girls for the home as well as teaching them sound Christian doctrine and morals. The Ursulines' first aim was to prepare future mothers, not nuns. Distinct from the spirit of the old monastic schooling of girls, Merici forbade anything peculiar to convent life in her schools. She instructed her fellow Ursulines "not to introduce anything that belongs to religious life" and she warned them against recruiting students to become nuns through persuasion "or by any tacit means."[15] Angela Merici's rule emphasized the *mother-idea* which meant teaching the children like "true and loving mothers" while caring for their bodies, hearts, and souls.[16]

The Ursulines became the largest of the orders founded for the education of girls in the sixteenth century. By the end of the next century, 320 Ursuline convents had been founded in France alone. Yet Merici's hopes of providing an education for domestic rather than monastic life failed to inspire her followers. In Ursuline academies the girls learned much about the wickedness of the world but little concerning the duties of a wife and mother. The Ursuline *Règlements* (1705) instructed the teachers often to remind the girls "that contempt of the world and its vanities is one of the essentials of the Christian life."[17] Not only was little domestic training offered in these academies, but the education was rudimentary. As a result of abundant religious instructions and devotions, the girls were prepared more for the convent than for the home. Indeed, the schedule followed by the girls in the Ursuline school closely resembled that of the nuns:

```
     6:30  Rise
     6:45  Morning Prayer
     7:00  Mass
8:00–10:00  Breakfast, Classes
    10:15  Litany
    10:30  Dinner
12:15–2:00  Reading aloud during meals, Recreation, Classes
     2:15  Prayer
     2:45  Lunch
     3:00  Classes
     4:15  Catechism
     6:45  Supper in silence, Recreation,
            Prayer and examination of conscience
     8:00  Retire
```

Other women also tried to educate girls for the home but failed. In the early seventeenth century, an Englishwoman, Mary Ward, headed a small group of her countrywomen at St. Omer. Ward believed that women played the chief role in family life and must be educated to assume it. She tried to provide the female equivalent of a Jesuit schooling, and incorporated religion, Latin, reading, writing, the native tongue, arithmetic, French, and Italian into her curriculum. The girls also learned needlework, nursing, and basic medicine. For Ward, a strong sound mental training would guarantee the faith of women and allow them to realize their potential. She insisted that women were not intellectually deficient.

> There is no such difference between men and women that women
> may not do great things, as we have seen by the example of many
> saints. And I hope to God it will be seen that women in time to
> come will do much. . . . As if we were in all things inferior to
> some other creatures which I suppose to be man.[19]

Rome suppressed Ward's group in 1631 for wearing secular dress, living outside the cloister and carrying out works "unsuitable to the womanliness of their sex, womanly modesty, and virginal purity."[20] The clergy needed and wanted women to prepare girls for their eventual roles as Christian homemakers yet they demanded that nuns live according to strict monastic rules. Removed as they were from the realities of secular life, it is not surprising that the nuns soon worried more about replenishing their ranks than preparing girls for the world. Thus, groups which began as reformers quickly succumbed to the fault they hoped to correct.

Despite the suppression of Ward's Institute, critics continued to complain that the existing convent schools failed to train girls for their roles as mothers and wives. Archbishop François Fénelon of Cambrai (1651-1715), the most influential of these critics, advised a noblewoman to educate her daughter at home rather than send her to a convent school. A bad convent harmed the morals of a girl while a good one left her ignorant of the world. Her shock and surprise when she returned home would lead her to believe that whatever was most wonderful had been hidden from her. "She leaves the convent like a person brought up in the darkness of a deep cavern who is suddenly taken out into the light of day."[21] A wise and religious mother should accustom her daughter gradually to the world.

Like Vives, Erasmus, Merici, and Ward, Fénelon insisted upon providing a better education for women in order to make them better wives and mothers. He designed a program of education which suited their future occupation. "The limits of a woman's learning—like that of a man— should be determined by her duties."[22] No woman should study politics, law, military art, philosophy, or theology. Instead, he recommended reading, writing, the four rules of arithmetic for keeping accounts, and a smattering of law in case of emergency. Finally, a woman must know how to do needlework, control children, manage estates, keep a neat house, and deal with servants.[23] Fénelon's ideal woman was a good housewife and manager, sound in character, and a faithful daughter of the church.[24]

At the same time Fénelon wrote *The Education of Girls*, Madame de Maintenon founded her famous school at Saint-Cyr. Influenced strongly by the archbishop, she sought to remedy the educational deficiency of French girls by training them for the world, not conventual life. Saint-Cyr's first prospectus outlined the Christian purposes of the school: to teach religion, inculcate piety, instill a horror of sin, and advocate the frequent reception of the sacraments. Yet Madame de Maintenon emphatically told the parents that though the school was religious she did not want the girls to take the veil. Instead, she wrote that the girls were educated as "seculars, good Christians," and that no "religious practices were demanded of them." Moreover, her students were "instructed in the duties of women in the 'world' and in all the conditions of life in which they may possibly find themselves."[25] At Saint-Cyr, the girls learned reading, writing, arithmetic, catechism, church singing, bible history, geography, dancing, music, needlework, and household tasks.[26]

Saint-Cyr was an extremely popular institution during the eighteenth century. Not only did this school become the model for curriculum, educational goals, and the ideal of preparing girls for family life, but its graduates profoundly influenced conventual life. As teachers and members of other religious orders, Madame de Maintenon's pupils carried on her educational philosophy. Yet Saint-Cyr, which founded its own religious order, the Dames of Saint-Louis, fell prey to the familiar pattern of training girls for the convent. Between its founding in 1686 and its closing in 1792 with the French Revolution, nearly 24% of its 2,900 students entered the convent.[27]

Saint-Cyr and the many convent schools affected by Madame de Maintenon's experiment combined the church's long-standing practice of educating women for consecrated virginity with the need to train them for domesticity. This tradition was carried to America where nuns immediately began schools that followed the French tradition of conventual education for girls.

Convent Schools in America, 1727–1860

Convent education, bearing the imprint of Madame de Maintenon and Archbishop Fénelon, was brought to America by the Ursulines in 1727. This religious order established a Catholic academy in New Orleans. In the early years the Ursulines taught reading, writing, arithmetic, catechism and industrial training and required daily prayers, mass, and examination of conscience. Their school grew from twenty-four boarders and forty day students in 1727 to 170 boarders in 1803, becoming the center of women's education in Louisiana and the neighboring territory.[28] A 1730 letter written by a priest in New Orleans described the feeling of the early Ursulines toward their work.

> There is not one of this holy community who is not delighted to have crossed the ocean, were she to do no other good save that of preserving these children in their innocence and of giving a polished and Christian education to young French girls who were in danger of being little better bred than slaves.[29]

The Ursulines' desire to provide a Christian and polished education characterized all the female religious orders who established convent schools, whether, like the Ursulines, they came from Europe, or whether they were founded in America. The nuns made extraordinary efforts to instill a deep religious faith and a fervent piety in their girls by placing religion at the center of the curriculum and requiring attendance at numerous services and devotions. Although there were differences in curricula, all Catholic girls' academies followed a monastic-like regimen. For example, pupils in the convent academy at Emmitsburg, Maryland led a life similar to that of their teachers, the American Sisters of Charity. They rose at 5:45, attended mass and prayers at 6:15, ate breakfast at 7:30, began classes at 8:00, recited the rosary at 11:30, ate dinner at 12:00, attended recreation at 12:30, went to adoration at 2:30, resumed classes at 3:00, studied and went to recreation at 5:00, ate supper and heard spiritual readings at 7:15, attended night prayers and retired.[30] The rules required total silence during all meals and from night prayers until after breakfast.

While convent schools aimed to produce devout, loyal Roman Catholics, they also tried to form cultured gentlewomen. The pupils learned proper manners and demeanor, drawing-room skills in music and art, and how to speak French with a natural accent. The French Sisters of Notre Dame de Namur explained in an 1841 advertisement for their Cincinnati academy that, "the heart must be educated as well as the mind and adorned with those qualities which beautify manners, and render virtue more attractive and amiable."[31] When Archbishop Gaetano Bedini, the Apostolic Delegate, visited the school in 1853, it numbered more than five hundred girls. The students addressed him in French, English, German, and Italian and he in turn spoke to the girls in French for nearly half an hour. Because so many of the children understood the language, no translator was needed.[32] Though facile and well-mannered, convent school girls' broad education was often superficial. Visitation Academy, opened in 1799 in Georgetown, offered the typical subjects of an American convent school. In 1836, its curriculum included:

> Religion Orthography, Reading, writing, Arithmetic, Grammar, English, Composition, Sacred and Profane History, Ancient and Modern Chronology, Mythology; most important and interesting experiments in Philosophy and Chemistry, Rhetoric, Versification, and Poetic Composition, Geography, Astronomy, the Use of Maps and Globes, French and Spanish Languages, Music on the Harp and Piano Forte, Vocal Music, Painting in Water Colours, Painting of Velvet, plain and ornamental Needlework, Tapestry, Lace Work or Embroidery on Bobbinet, Bead Work, and Domestic Economy.[33]

Fervent piety, modest demeanor, and artistic skills meant more in the convent-school world than academic proficiency. This kind of education trained girls to be Catholic gentlewomen whose future choices were confirmed to the convent or cultured, devout motherhood.

While nuns held fast to the traditional Catholic concept of women's education, non-Catholic educational reformers in early nineteenth-century America sought to rid women's education of ornamental accomplishments, substituting instead solid academic subjects. They strongly believed in the intellectual capacity of women and the importance of channelling their talents into the productive area of teaching. Reformers believed that as mothers or teachers, women must actively promote virtue in those around them and in society as a whole. Important early girls' schools which held this philosophy included Sarah Pierce's Academy in Litchfield

(1791), Joseph Emerson's Ladies Seminary in Connecticut (1818), Troy Seminary (1821), Ipswich Female Seminary (1828), Hartford (1823), and Mount Holyoke (1837).[34]

Influential female reformers headed many of these academies. Emma Willard, who founded Troy Seminary in 1821, sought to provide an education that would make the girls self-sufficient. Although Willard adhered to the idea of separate spheres of activity for men and women and the ideology of domesticity, she strongly believed in women's capacity for intellectual excellence. In her academy girls prepared for a profession, and many became teachers.[35]

Like the nuns who staffed convent academies, many reformers placed great emphasis on religion. At Ipswich Seminary, Zilpah Grant and Mary Lyon banned music, painting, and French in favor of the sciences, mathematics, theology, and philosophy.[36] Later, Lyon moved to Mount Holyoke, where her evangelical religiosity and unshakeable belief in the capacity of women to excel spiritually, intellectually, and physically deeply affected and inspired female students. Many converted and became missionary teachers, committed to saving America and the world.[37]

One of the most influential female educators and writers in the nineteenth century was Catherine Beecher. Her work at Hartford Seminary, which she established in 1828, convinced her of the need for reform in women's education. She argued that the number and variety of subjects offered in the female academy's curriculum encouraged superficiality and detracted from substantial education. After publishing her suggestions for reform in 1829, she opened the Western Female Institute in Cincinnati in 1833. Because Beecher saw women as the "educators of the human mind, the nurse of the sick, the guardian of infancy, and the conservator of the domestic state," she sought to educate women for the roles of nurse, housewife, and teacher.[38] Though Beecher confined women to their traditional professions, she tried to overcome their marginal status. Her ideology placed women in the center of national life, which for her was the home and the family.[39]

These female educational reformers never questioned

the accepted nineteenth-century ideal "true womanhood," which glorified piety, purity, obedience, and domesticity. Like the nuns, the women placed piety first in their educational goals. Unlike the nuns, they also stressed learning. Catholic academies, on the other hand, gave the girls little training for work inside or outside the home and showed little concern for the practical issue of a woman supporting herself or the domestic duties of a wife and mother. Like the Ursulines and Saint-Cyr's teachers, American sisters worried most about the souls of their pupils and the manners, demeanor, and pastimes that would not endanger their chances for heaven. One sister teaching in America explained her interest in the spiritual welfare of her students:

> A Sister of Providence cannot go to heaven alone; if she is not surrounded by the souls she had brought to the knowledge and love of God, she will not find the way herself to the celestial abode. God in calling us to the religious life wished not only our own sanctification but He called us to work with Him for the sanctification of our brethren; thus only shall we sanctify ourselves.[40]

In a country where influential and prominent girls' schools prepared their students for the moral reform of America and the world, Catholic academies prepared their pupils for eternal life.

The Religious Orders 2

Introduction

*A*merican Catholic girls in the nineteenth and twentieth centuries received their educations from women who belonged to all-female religious communities. These teachers lived very differently from any other women in American society. Not only did they take vows of poverty, chastity, and obedience, but they held values that set them apart from the larger Catholic community. To understand the schooling of American Catholic girls, it is necessary to examine the growth of female religious communities, their lifestyle and ethos and the history of the particular orders which staffed the academies under study in this work.

Growth of Female Religious Orders in America

European orders of sisters viewed America as a vast field for missionary endeavor. Superiors of religious communities sent colony after colony of teachers to the New World. Between 1790 and 1920, 119 European orders established foundations in America, and 8 Canadian communities came to the United States. In the same period 38 American orders were also founded.

American bishops needed the services of these women in order to establish Catholic schools. From colonial times well into the nineteenth century, American public schools reflected Protestant values. Bishops believed that unless Catholic schools were organized, the future of American Catholicism would be jeopardized. John Carroll, the first American bishop, implored the contemplative Discalced Carmelite nuns of Port Tobacco, Maryland, to expand their apostolate to include teaching. When requesting a dispensation from their rule, he wrote: "Their convent would be a far greater benefit in the future if a school for the training of girls in piety and learning were begun by them."[1] Rome agreed with Carroll but the nuns refused to come out of seclusion.

TABLE 1			
European and American Foundations of Religious Orders			
	1790–1829	1830–1859	1860–1900	1900–1920
American	5	11	12	10
European	7	28	47	37
Canadian			8	
Total	12	39	67	47

SOURCE: Elenor T. Dehey, *Religious Orders of Women in the United States.* (Indiana: W. B. Conkey, 1930.)

Though this particular community survived, few contemplative groups were successful in a country which desperately needed sisters engaged in the active apostolate. Growth and prosperity came to those groups of sisters who carried their religious ideals into the world instead of keeping them behind a grille.

Female religious communities grew very rapidly in nineteenth-century America.[2] In 1822 there were roughly two hundred sisters in the United States. By 1920 the figure had jumped to 88,773.

	1822	1834	1840	1845	1850	1860	1870	1880	1890	1895	1900	1905	1910	1915	1920

TABLE 2

Number of Nuns and Convents in America 1822–1920

	1822	1834	1840	1845	1850	1860	1870	1880	1890	1895	1900	1905	1910	1915	1920
Convents	12	45	71	82	158	381	906	2154	2824	3646	4054	4569	5310	6513	7397
Nuns	200	488	700	1108	1664	4005	9513	22617	29652	37159	44542	52123	64552	78159	88773

SOURCE: *The Laity's Directory to the Church Services* (New York: William H. Creagh, 1822); *The United States Catholic Almanac or Laity's Directory* (Baltimore: J. Myres, 1834); *The Metropolitan Catholic Almanac and Laity's Directory* (Baltimore: Fielding Lucas, 1838–1857); *American Catholic Almanac and List of Clergy* (New York: Ed. Dunigan Bros., 1858); *Metropolitan Catholic Almanac and Laity's Directory* (Baltimore: John Murphy and Co., 1859–1860); *Sadlier's Catholic Almanac and Ordo* (New York: D. and J. Sadlier, 1864–1894); *Hoffman's Catholic Directory* (Milwaukee: M. H. Wiltzins & Co., 1895–1899); *Catholic Directory, Almanac and Clergy List* (Milwaukee: M. H. Wilt-zins and Co., 1900–1911); *The Official Catholic Directory and Clergy List* (New York: P. J. Kennedy & Sons, 1912–1920), hereinafter to be cited as the *Catholic Directories*.

Note: The figures in these directories are not always reliable but they provide the only source for the number of sisters in America. Each diocese listed the number of priests, and many directories contained a general survey of Catholicity in the United States that included the total number of American clergy; yet few dioceses indicated the number of sisters. I obtained my figures by counting the number of sisters in every Catholic institution mentioned in these directories from 1822 to 1890. After 1890 the directories listed each female religious order and their number. I added the number of each community to reach my figures for the years 1895 to 1920. The number of convents was obtained by counting each convent listed in every diocese in the country from 1822 to 1920. My figures are not exact for a variety of reasons. Some communities listed their total number in their motherhouse figures and then listed the number of sisters in individual convents in another part of the directory. Other communities included postulants and novices while many only listed professed sisters. Though my calculations are rough, they are the closest that can be obtained given the source material.

The sisters nursed and did social work but their primary interest was education. They staffed elementary schools and opened their own private female academies, which provided the only Catholic secondary education available to Catholic girls until the turn of the century.[3] The growth of academies was nothing short of phenomenal: from 47 schools in 1840 to 709 by 1910.

TABLE 3

Catholic Girls' Academies in America, 1840–1910

	1840	1850	1860	1870	1880	1885	1890	1895	1900	1905	1910
Academies	47	91	202		511	581	624	609	662	692	709

SOURCE: *Catholic Directories*, 1840–1910.

NOTE: Figures unavailable for 1870.

Although the extraordinary increase in the number of academies was significant for the development of Roman Catholicism throughout America, their growth in the raw, frontier cities and towns of the Midwest was especially important. With few rivals in the educational field, the sisters' schools were welcomed by both Catholics and Protestants.They not only provided training in academic subjects but taught Old World manners and culture or at least a veneer of them to the daughters of those aspiring to gentility.[4] Sisters established their academies in well-populated places where they were certain to draw large numbers of students to their schools. The four religious orders under study founded convent schools in such areas in the Midwest: Chicago, Dubuque, Cincinnati, St. Louis, and Davenport. The figures from these dioceses in Table 4 show the parallel growth of nuns and academies as well as the large numbers of girls educated in these schools.

Religious orders grew at such a rapid rate and academies were established because American Catholic women were attracted to the lifestyle and ideals of the sisters. Convents offered their members power, respect, and a significant occupation at a time when women in secular society were experiencing a relative deterioration in status due to the nineteenth-century shift of economic production from the

TABLE 4

Growth of Nuns, Academies and Students
in Selected Midwestern Dioceses, 1860–1920

	1860	1865	1870	1875	1880	1885	1890	1895	1900	1905	1910	1915
CHICAGO												
Convents				31			77	143	171	218	232	
Nuns	150	142	142				1063	1015		2246		
Priests		65	96	142	196	215	288	323	389	459	648	688
Academies		3	8	11	13	15	19	22	15	19	28	22
Number in Academies	156			1509	2062	1767	2407	2727	2013	2843	4265	5100

	1860	1865	1870	1875	1880	1885	1890	1895	1900	1905	1910	1915
TABLE 4 Continued												
CINCINNATI												
Convents							109	118	120	131	143	
Nuns					988		1399					
Priests	112		131	160	168	216	226	224	259	312	354	356
Academies	11	7	1	12	12	8	9	11	11	12	12	14
Number in Academies						732	740	954	980	1500	1753	1903
DAVENPORT												
Convents						5	39	39	46	53	52	
Nuns						165		277				
Priests						76	91	101	116	125	113	
Academies						6	6	7	7	7	7	
Number in Academies						930		800	950	1200	1217	1445
DUBUQUE												
Convents	6		12		57		68	112	125	96	105	
Nuns	122				446							
Priests	56	58	80	135	208	147	187	240	273	216	237	
Academies	6	8	8	6	18	14	15	13	15	13	15	11
Number in Academies		1500	1500	600	2194	1913	2794	1757	2785	2290	2670	2446
ST. LOUIS												
Convents	26		35		91	91	115	128	142	168	184	
Nuns					1033							
Priests	120	120	180	214	260	254	213	335	418	484	514	526
Academies		9	9	9	7	15	15	14	18	18	22	17
Number in Academies					684	901	1082	2124	1800	2000	5000	1781

SOURCE: *Catholic Directories*, 1860–1920.

NOTE: These figures, like those in Table 2, are not completely reliable. They should be viewed as approximate. The absence of figures in various places in the tables means that the Catholic Directories for that year did not supply the information. In addition, the reader might be interested to know that all the dioceses under study educated many more Catholic girls than boys. Appendix A provides the number of colleges and boys enrolled in them for the dioceses of Chicago, Cincinnati, Davenport, and St. Louis.

household to the factory.[5] Religious life also freed women from the probability of subordination to men in marriage, the pain and danger of childbirth and the drudgeries of domestic duties required to maintain a family. These pragmatic reasons combined with a devotional revival in the Roman Catholic Church to produce a large number of female vocations.[6] Yet the many and varied factors which attracted women to religious life mattered little once they entered the convent. Their lives, their hopes, and their needs were no longer their own but those of the community. The next section describes the way of life and the goal of those who chose the convent.

The Common Life

Although female religious communities differed in origin, cultural composition and government, American Catholic sisters shared the same lifestyle and ideals. Ideally, they all left the world in a quest for spiritual perfection and union with God. The religious communities these women joined provided the structures through which they might reach their goals.

When a woman entered a community she became a postulant for six months to a year; then, a novice for one to two years. During this period of initial formation, the applicant tested her vocation under the guidance of a mistress of novices. She learned the customs of the order, the meaning of the vows, methods of prayer and the demeanor of a nun. Rigorous and often unpleasant, this experience was designed to make or break the candidate. If the woman successfully completed this training, she took temporary vows of poverty, chastity, and obedience. After spending a number of years living and working with the community, she was allowed to make a final profession of vows.

Assenting to poverty meant pledging oneself to contentment with the mere necessities of life and disengagement from an interest in worldly things. All goods belonged to the community and the sisters held no individual possessions. Some orders set aside a day on which the nuns were required to lay everything that had been given them for their use at the feet of the superior, thus reminding them of their poverty. In other communities, superiors examined the cells of the sisters to discover whether the nuns had any possessions that they had not received permission to use.

The most stringent warnings in convent rules concerned chastity, the "angelic virtue." Chastity referred not only to the absence of sexual intercourse but every aspect of a sister's conduct. She must always be vigilant about this most precious gift and keep close guard on all her senses. Because men posed the greatest threat to a nun's virtue, the rules forbade any unnecessary contact or familiarity with the opposite sex. The *Rule of St. Augustine*, used by many female communities, warned against men.

> Let there be nothing in your gait, in your manner, in your dress or in any of your movements, which can tempt any one to evil; but let your whole demeanor be such as becomes the sanctity of your state. If your eyes light upon any man, let them never be fixed upon him. When you go out, you are not forbidden to see men, but to try to attract them or wish to be admired by them, is criminal. For not only by touch, but by affection, and by looks also, mutual concupiscence arises.[7]

The sisters continually watched each other when men were present. One who so much as "fixed her gaze" upon a man received admonitions and penance.

The last vow required complete obedience to the rules and constitutions of the order and to the superior. Whether important or trivial, agreeable or disagreeable, a sister immediately obeyed her superior, humbly and without complaint or murmur. A good sister believed that when she obeyed her superior, she followed the will of God.

To help the sisters keep their vows, a tight schedule regulated every moment of the day. Their horarium revolved around religious exercises. Each day they recited morning prayers or the divine office together, meditated, heard mass, listened to spiritual readings during meals, said the rosary, attended night prayers, examined their consciences, did spiritual reading, and went to evening chapel. They received the sacrament of penance weekly and made a retreat once a year. A passage from the constitutions of the Sinsinawa Dominicans reflected the attitudes of religious communities toward the fulfilment of spiritual duties.

> But, although perfection exists in the interior of the soul, the Sisters will vainly persuade themselves that they can acquire it by neglecting the exterior exercises of the spiritual life. The Saints themselves, with all their acquired virtues, took long hours from apostolic labors to spend in the affairs of God.[8]

Along with vows and schedules, numerous rules governed the lives of the sisters. They observed silence at all times in their convents except during an hour of daily recreation. Even when teaching they avoided unnecessary conversation with each other and especially with visitors. If absolute necessity demanded speech, a sister spoke in a very low voice and as briefly as possible. The nuns ate their meals in silence and listened to spiritual reading. Superiors inspected in-coming and out-going mail as well as all reading material. When a sister went to the parlor to receive a visitor, another sister accompanied her. She could speak to no man alone, except a priest in the confessional. The rules also discouraged conversations with laywomen. Rather than pleasure, a sister should feel mortified when obliged to speak with seculars. The Sinsinawa Dominicans' constitutions reminded the sisters of the impression they should leave with visitors.

> Seculars coming from the company of a Sister should carry with them the conviction that Religious are the happiest and the holiest persons in the world, and that they are truly deserving of full confidence in the education of young girls.[9]

Female communities regulated relations among the sisters themselves. All forbade "particular friendships" which were seen as disruptive and divisive in community life.[10] According to the directives regulating the lives of the Sisters of Mercy, the love and union of religious persons should be

> founded not on flesh and blood, or any human motive, but on God alone; as their hearts should be united together in Jesus Christ, their Spouse and Redeemer in whom and for whom they should live and love one another, the Sisters of this Institute

20

should not admit any particular friendships, attachments, or affections among them, and shall studiously avoid all private parties and unions, as the source of discords and division, and as hostile to purity of heart, to charity, and the spirit of Religion.[11]

The Sisters of Charity of the B.V.M. prohibited the sisters from touching one another without necessity. The circumstances under which the B.V.M.'s could express affection were also strictly regulated. Nuns were allowed to kiss each other on vow days, to mark returns after long absences, or in an effort toward reconciliation. The B.V.M.'s, however, were forbidden to kiss each other in church, on the street, or in any public place.[12]

Communities maintained strict observance of rules through a custom known as a chapter of faults. During a weekly assembly, each nun prostrated herself before the superior and recited a list of the "exterior faults" she had committed against the rules and constitutions of her community. The sisters were enjoined to report the slightest infraction against the rule, and penances were based on the gravity of the fault.

Convent life was often far from pleasant. Not only did most nuns live under spartan conditions but they were occasionally subject to harsh local superiors who overstepped their authority. Officials from the motherhouses reprimanded unjust superiors and sometimes removed them from power. In addition, all convents were plagued by individuals who disrupted community life by their pettiness, selfishness, bad tempers, inflexibility, pride and inability to get along with others. Some women proved unfit for religious life and were dismissed. Others suffered nervous breakdowns and were sent to sanitariums or retired to the motherhouse.

The difficulty of sustaining community life was compounded by the fact that the nuns were not related by blood, nor were they permitted close friendships. The rules of every religious community commanded the women to love one another as Jesus loved them and to practice charity at all times. The sisters must guard against anger and beg forgiveness of those they offended. In order to reduce the inevitable tensions and frictions arising in a single-sex household with little privacy or room for individuality, the sisters were constantly reminded to avoid anything in their conduct, manners or conversation that would disturb the union of the convent. Janet Erskine Stuart, one of the Society of the Sacred Heart's greatest educators and superior general from 1911 to her death in 1914, reminded her sisters that peculiarities and eccentricities were not sinful but unbecoming because they drew others away from God by distracting them. Nuns should correct their own oddities.

> It is more necessary for us than for other people to pay attention to the avoidance of oddities. In the world people get their corners rubbed off, but in Religion, we are treated with so much kindness, no one ever laughs at our defects so that they might easily develop.[13]

Despite the faults of the sisters, the breaking of vows and rules, and the unhappiness present in some communities, convent life remained attractive to thousands of American women. Given the difficulties of religious life, the unmeasurable quality of spirituality appeared to be the cement which held it together. One sister wrote at the turn of the century about her years in the convent.

> It were better to pass over the scenes of parting from father and mother, brothers and sisters and home, the only world I knew. It will be enough to say that I have never regretted the step, and that all that I hoped for,—and much more—has been given to me—verily the hundred-fold.[14]

Convent spirituality gave the hundred-fold to some, but to most it provided a satisfying way of dealing with unfair superiors, petty rules, uncomfortable clothing, poor food, overwork, and loneliness. Women who entered the convent seeking perfection and union with Jesus viewed suffering and pain as opportunities for a closer imitation of their savior. Few novice mistresses or superiors failed to remind their charges to look at the cross and meditate upon the passion and death of Jesus when conditions seemed unbearable. The harder the life meant the greater the sacrifice and the greater the reward. Whatever its merits or demerits, this system was

useful in producing an extraordinarily self-sacrificing, disci-
plined, motivated, and hard-working corps of teachers for
the Church.

The large number of women who joined or stayed in
religious life attested to the success of community life. Without an increase in vocations, religious orders could not have
grown, prospered, and accomplished so much. The ability of
convents to keep their recruits is illustrated in the following
table for the midwestern order, the Sinsinawa Dominicans.
Except for the unstable early years of the community, only a
small number who entered the Sinsinawa Dominicans left.

	1847 to 1859	1860 to 1869	1870 to 1879	1880 to 1889	1890 to 1899	1900 to 1905	1906 to 1910	1911 to 1915
Entered	24	46	105	164	197	186	167	173
Remained	13	39	91	146	177	165	146	147
Left	11	7	14	18	20	21	21	26
Age of those Remaining	21	22.9	23.8	24.3	25.1	26.3	23.7	24.3
Age of those Leaving	21.7	20.4	20.9	22.1	25.2	24	26	24.8

TABLE 5

The Number and Ages of Sinsinawa Dominicans Who Entered,
Remained and Left, 1847–1915

SOURCE: Record of Entrants and Departures for the Sinsinawa Dominicans, 1847 to Present.
(AOP).

The Religious Orders

Although united by a common lifestyle and ideal, teaching communities of sisters in America were distinguished
from one another in history, spirit, and membership. In order
to discover whether these differences affected the schooling
they gave to American Catholic girls, it is necessary to ana-
lyze particular communities. The following section compares
the foundations of the four groups of teaching sisters under
study in this work, their attitudes toward education, and

their preparation for teaching. These groups are the Society of the Sacred Heart, the Sisters of Mercy of Chicago (Mercies), the Sisters of Charity of the Blessed Virgin Mary (B.V.M.'s), and the Sinsinawa Dominicans. They were chosen because they were important and well-known orders who dominated female Catholic education in the Midwest. All were founded in the nineteenth century, established academies and parochial schools throughout the country, and possessed excellent reputations as teachers. These orders were regarded as among the best-educated sisters in America. They also differed significantly in origin, development, government, and wealth. Together, these groups can be viewed as representative of the various religious orders who educated American girls.

The Society of the Sacred Heart

Founded in France in 1800, the Society of the Sacred Heart became one of the most influential and important religious orders of women in the Roman Catholic Church. An international order, the Society quickly spread throughout Europe and sent colonies to North America, New Zealand, Australia, South America, Central America, and the Orient. It concentrated upon boading schools for the "better classes" and attracted wealthy and powerful Catholics wherever it established schools. Sacred Heart schools also served as a model for the schools of other orders. No other group of Catholic women rivalled the influence of the Society on the schooling of Catholic girls in the nineteenth and twentieth centuries.

The history and character of the Society is inseparable from that of its founder, Madeleine Sophie Barat (1779–1865). Daughter of a Burgundian barrel-maker, Barat never attended school but was tutored by her brother, a seminarian and teacher in the local boys' school. She pursued the same classical course as the boys in Louis Barat's school, learning Greek, Latin, mathematics, scripture, modern languages, history, literature, botany, and astronomy. After a two year imprisonment during the French Revolution, Louis Barat took his

24

seventeen-year old sister with him to Paris, where she completed her studies. For four years she read theology, scripture, the early fathers, and mystical writings of the saints.[15]

Madeleine Sophie Barat hoped to enter a Carmelite monastery when the convents in France reopened after the French Revolution. But she met Father Joseph Varin, leader of the Fathers of the Sacred Heart, a group which awaited the re-establishment of the Jesuits. He found in Barat a natural leader for the female religious order he planned to establish. Under Varin's protection, Barat and three other young women joined together in 1800 to help rechristianize France through the education of young girls.

Until Barat and Varin constructed a rule and constitution, the little group followed a summary of the rule of St. Ignatius. Rome approved the constitutions in 1826 and placed the Society under the protection of the Holy See. The Society was strictly governed by its superior general, Madeleine Sophie Barat, who ruled from a central headquarters in Paris with assistance from advisors.

While the Society was establishing itself in Europe and gaining Roman approval, Bishop Louis DuBourg of Louisiana asked Barat for missionaries to his diocese. She selected Philippine Duchesne, (1769–1852), daughter of a wealthy Grenoble family, to head the small group of nuns who arrived in the New World in 1818. From their first foundation in St. Charles, Missouri, the Society expanded to Grand Coteau, Louisiana, (1821), St. Louis, (1827), New York City, (1841), McSherrytown, Pennsylvania, (1842), Philadelphia, (1847), Buffalo, (1849), Detroit, (1851), Albany, (1852), Chicago, (1858), Cincinnati, (1869), Providence, (1872), Boston, (1880), Omaha, (1881), San Francisco, (1887), and Seattle, (1907).

The Society's rapid expansion throughout the United States did not weaken the bonds between American and European members of the order. American Religious of the Sacred Heart maintained a balance between French and American ways by adapting to local conditions while preserving many of their traditions. Barat set the tone for the

Society in America when Philippine Duchesne worried about her failure to observe part of the rule. Duchesne wrote to Barat:

> As to enclosure, there is not a wall within a thousand miles of here; and wooden fences keep out animals, but not men. Our enclosure consists in remaining at home, but people come into our grounds as much as they like, making an entrance anywhere.[16]

From the Paris motherhouse Barat wrote her daughters to reassure them of the necessity to dispense with parts of the rule at certain times. Barat's attitude toward adaptation, the constant communciation between the motherhouse and the American nuns, and the frequent arrival of French-trained Religious kept the Society in America acutely aware of its European connections.

Most important, though, for the worldwide unity of the Society was its common ministry of educating the upper classes. Academies for the elite constituted the central work of the Society. Barat wrote:

> Usually we succeed with the upper classes and we should hold to this all the more since the education of the other classes is taken care of by a number of religious orders whose aim is precisely that type of education.[17]

In America wealthy Catholics and non-Catholics sent their daughters to the academies of the Sacred Heart. These schools also received special attention from American bishops, cardinals, and Jesuits. Other female orders resented the Sacred Heart academies, even though they imitated their system. Some laypeople and clergy also disliked what they called the pretensions of the Society and the aristocratic nature of its schools. In 1866, three liberal priests of the New York Archdiocese, Richard Burtsell, Stephen McGlynn, and Thomas Preston, visited Manhattanville, a Sacred Heart Academy in New York. Burtsell recounted some of the grievances that the clergy held against the Society.

> The Sisters of the Sacred Heart are haughty in their ways: and too cool towards common priests to be popular among the secular clergy. They only think Jesuits worthy of their esteem. They present the Archbishop with a gift on exhibition-day: last year they

gave him a $1000 cross. . . . Fr. Preston was the chaplain of the Sacred Heart. A bishop, vicar-general, or Jesuit was invited to say mass on any extraordinary festival. Mad. Hardie pretended not to know Fr. Preston after five years that he had been to see them. Fr. Preston considers them haughty sisters without religious spirit.[18]

The Society recognized the criticism and resentment directed toward them. Madame E. Ten Broeck, R.S.C.J., wrote to Father Daniel Hudson on the subject of Sacred Heart convent schools in 1890.

> As to the "*Sacre Coeur*" and our methods, we are not so conceited, or ill-informed as to imagine ourselves superior in any respect to other orders. But the Bishops always invite us for what they especially style the "Upper Class of Catholics," hence in our Academies for young Ladies we are supposed to be forming daughters of gentlemen in America, or "New Ireland," not Teachers.[19]

Despite the criticisms, the Society of the Sacred Heart set the standard for the education of American Catholic girls.

The Sisters of Mercy

In their European foundation and worldwide expansion, the Sisters of Mercy resembled the Society of the Sacred Heart. Unlike the Society and the other two orders under study, the Mercies trained nurses and social workers as well as teachers. Moreover, they had no central government. Because the Mercy order was organized on a diocesean basis, convents were under the authority of local bishops. This combination of independent foundations and varied works made the Mercies very attractive to bishops and helped the Mercies become the largest female religious community in the world.

Catherine McAuley (1787–1841), the founder of the Sisters of Mercy, was a well-to-do, forty-three-year-old Dublin heiress who purchased property on Baggot Street and began construction of a kind of social service center. The house opened in 1827 as a school for poor and working girls, and a refuge for orphans and unemployed servants. In 1828 McAuley and two other laywomen moved into Baggot Street and began visiting the sick. They attracted many influential and wealthy helpers and supporters.

27

Unlike Madeleine Sophie Barat, McAuley originally aimed to establish a group of Catholic social workers, not a religious order. In her first mission at Baggot Street, she made it a definite point to avoid association with nuns.[20] At the same time she and her helpers began calling themselves the Sisters of Mercy, adopted a common dress and led the life of a community. They assembled each morning for meditation and prayers, attended mass, said the rosary in common, and met again for night prayers.

McAuley's little group needed a rule to live by. Archbishop Daniel Murray of Dublin encouraged the sisters to adapt to their needs the rule of the Presentation Sisters, another recently founded Irish order. The most important changes by the Sisters of Mercy were the inclusion of chapters regarding visiting the sick and modification of the rule of enclosure in order to remove any obstacles to this visitation. The first chapter of the rule and constitutions clearly spelled out the object of the Institute of the Sisters of Mercy.

> The Sisters admitted to this Religious Congregation, besides attending particularly to their own perfection, which is the principal end of all Religious Orders, should also have in view what is peculiarly characteristic of this Institute—that is, a most serious application to the Instruction of Poor Girls, Visitation of the Sick, and Protection of Distressed Women of good character.[21]

The sisters submitted their rule and constitution to Rome in 1837 and four years later received approval.

While the Mercies struggled to establish themselves as a religious order, McAuley, like Barat, was visited by American bishops asking for sisters to organize convents in their dioceses. In 1843 McAuley sent six sisters to the Pittsburgh diocese of Bishop Michael O'Connor. Frances Warde (1810–1884), a member of a wealthy and politically and clerically well-connected Irish family, headed this group of missionaries. Under her leadership the Mercies quickly spread across the United States, establishing convents throughout New England, the Midwest, the Middle Atlantic states, California, and Florida. Unlike the Society of the Sacred Heart, the Mercies never had to balance between the traditions and rules of the Irish motherhouse and the needs of the American church. Since each foundation was independent, they adapted thoroughly and with little hesitation to local conditions when required.

Warde made her earliest and probably most important foundation in Chicago. At the request of Bishop William Quarter, the Mercies in 1846 became the first Catholic sisters to establish a convent in the city. Impressed by the needs of poor immigrant Catholics, the Sisters of Mercy laid the groundwork for Catholic educational and charitable institutions in Chicago. Within two weeks of arrival they opened a free school and private academy for girls, modelled on the Mercy academy in Pittsburgh. They immediately began visiting the sick, the poor, and the imprisoned. In 1849 they nursed victims of a cholera epidemic and opened a home for children who had been orphaned as a result of the epidemic. Two years later, they took over the care of Chicago's first hospital, Illinois General, which became Mercy Hospital in 1853. The nuns opened the first five parochial schools in Chicago, the first evening school for Catholic adults, the first convert class, and the first working girls' home.

Not until 1856, ten years after their arrival, were the Mercies joined in Chicago by another group of religious. In this first decade in Chicago, the Mercy order increased in number from five to thirty-five nuns. Considering that many nuns died from contagious diseases and overwork, these figures were impressive indeed. Of the original five members, for example, four had died by 1854. The first died of consumption in 1848, the second of cholera in 1849. Two years later, hard frontier conditions caused the demise of the third. Then, in 1854 another cholera epidemic took the life of the superior, Agatha O'Brien, as well as three more sisters.

Despite the extraordinary efforts of the Mercies, they became embroiled in a number of serious disputes with their bishops. The sisters and the bishops often held very different views on the extent of ecclesiastical power over the order.[22] Their subjection to the bishop, though, also had a positive side. Unlike other orders, the Mercies were not torn between remaining faithful to the Irish motherhouse and responding to the needs of the local church. More than any of the communities under study, the Sisters of Mercy of Chicago identified with the diocese and concentrated all their resources there.

The Sisters of Charity of the Blessed Virgin Mary

When the first members of the Sisters of Charity of the Blessed Virgin Mary began their work, they differed in many ways from the Society of the Sacred Heart and the Mercies. The B.V.M.'s were founded in Dublin by four young, poor, ill-educated Irish women: Mary Frances Clarke, Margaret Mann, Rose O'Toole, and Eliza Kelly. In 1831 they began to live together as a community and a few months later they opened a small school. With no guidance from the clergy or experience in religious life, they decided to become a religious order. Having heard that the children of Irish immigrants in Philadelphia needed religious instruction, these four women came to this city in 1833.

Within a few days after their arrival, the B.V.M.'s met an Irish priest, Terence Donaghoe (1795–1869), who immediately gained their trust. He engaged them for his parish school and became their director and reverend superior. In 1842 Bishop Matthew Loras of Dubuque requested five B.V.M.'s for his diocese. Instead, all nineteen members came to Dubuque.

By 1845 the community had adopted a rule which declared that the "principal end" of the B.V.M.'s was to honor the Holy Family: Jesus, Mary, and Joseph. Although the "principal object" of the new order was the perfection and salvation of the nuns' souls, they endeavored to honor the sacred childhood of Jesus Christ by instructing girls

> whose hearts they are called to form to the love of God, in the practice of every virtue and knowledge of Religion; whilst at the same time they sow the seeds of useful knowledge and prepare them to be good members of society.[23]

In accordance with their rule, the B.V.M.'s immediately opened a boarding school for girls in Dubuque and sent a second group of nuns to Davenport, Iowa, in 1844 to establish an academy. The order attracted new recruits from nearby farming towns and the increase in vocations enabled the B.V.M.'s to open schools throughout Iowa. In 1867 they came to Chicago's Holy Family parish. Arnold Damen, S.J., pastor of Holy Family, thought these women ideal for teaching the children of Irish immigrants since the sisters were Irish-born or from Irish families in rural Iowa. Going to Chicago broadened the group: it consequently expanded in the nineteenth century to Minnesota, northern Illinois, Milwaukee, Kansas City, and San Francisco.

Two years after the B.V.M.'s opened a school in Chicago, Fr. Donaghoe, their director, died. He was succeeded by Mary Frances Clarke (1806–1887), one of the original four members. Under her leadership the B.V.M.'s received Roman approval in 1877 and became a pontifical congregation. This meant that the B.V.M.'s, like the Society of the Sacred Heart, were governed from a central headquarters and subject directly to Rome instead of the local bishop. The order used this independence to expand without restriction, opening more schools and gaining more recruits than the other three groups.

The Sinsinawa Dominicans

The youngest of the four religious communities under study and the only one founded in America is the Sinsinawa Dominicans. They began their work just a few miles east of the B.V.M. motherhouse and during the same period that the B.V.M.'s moved to Dubuque. Like the Society of the Sacred Heart and the B.V.M.'s and unlike the Mercies, the Sinsinawa Dominicans were established primarily for the purpose of teaching.

Samuel Mazzuchelli (1814–1864), an Italian Dominican missionary priest, founded the Sinsinawa Dominicans. This well-educated son of a rich Milanese banker came to America in 1828, settling in Dubuque in 1835. Nine years later he purchased Sinsinawa Mound in southwestern Wisconsin, where he established a college for boys. Needing sisters to teach in his primary school and work as housekeepers for the priests and students of the college, Mazzuchelli wrote the Dominican Fathers in Ohio to request Dominican sisters. In 1846 he asked Father Donaghoe across the river for some B.V.M.'s to staff his school.

> We shall be in need of some good persons to keep school to the girls of this parish, and to do all the sewing and mending of our house which will be considerable this winter. A suitable place below the road opposite the church will be shortly fitted up for that purpose.[24]

Unsuccessful in both attempts, Mazzuchelli was forced to found his own female community. His first recruits were Mary McNulty, a district school teacher and Mary Routtan, a former nurse. Both women had been Daughters of Charity in Cincinnati. McNulty had left after the expiration of her vows while Routtan had been secularized. By 1848 seven women had joined Mazzuchelli's new community, enabling the Italian priest to staff small parish schools and a private day school at Sinsinawa.

The Sinsinawa Dominicans experienced grave difficulties in their early years. Wracked by internal strife, ten of the original fifteen members left the order. The first two recruits, Mary McNulty and Mary Routtan quit the Dominicans in 1849.[25] McNulty attempted to disband the community but failed when the nuns agreed to abide by the decision of the youngest member, who insisted they remain together. In addition, Mazzuchelli's 1849 decision to resign as president of Sinsinawa College and relinquish control of the sisters, compounded the problems of the young community. Without Mazzuchelli's protection, the sisters became servants for the college and were able to staff only one small school.

After withdrawing to Benton, a small town near Sinsinawa, Samuel Mazzuchelli realized the plight of the sisters left behind. He wrote to the Dominican provincial in 1850.

> I am sorry that the four most excellent sisters will be kept there [at the College] mainly as servants, and the schools of the country are without Christian education. Those sisters were not to be employed all the time in such hard work.[26]

The sisters followed Mazzuchelli to Benton in 1852, where they established St. Clara Academy. They also began to staff schools in the little towns nearby. After fifteen years in Benton, during which time the community stabilized, the nuns returned to Sinsinawa Mound and built a motherhouse and academy. Following the election of Sister Emily Power (1844–1909) as superior in 1867, the Sinsinawa Dominicans embarked on a program of expansion. During Mother Emily's forty-two-year tenure, the order spread throughout Wisconsin, into Illinois, Minnesota, and other parts of the Midwest. Like the B.V.M.'s, the Sinsinawa Dominicans taught primarily in parish schools, but they also opened many academies.

The Sinsinawa Dominicans' mission to teach was clearly outlined in their rule of 1860, which Father Mazzuchelli formulated. Although the rule provided for self-government, it placed the order under the jurisdiction of the local bishop. After Mazzuchelli's death in 1864, the sisters realized the need for a rule and constitutions that would make them a pontifical congregation like the Society of the Sacred Heart and the B.V.M.'s. They also longed for a stronger Dominican identity. In 1877 Emily Power, leader of the Sinsinawa Dominicans, journeyed to Rome to discuss this issue with the Dominican vicar-general, Joseph San Vito. He suggested they adapt the constitutions of a group of English Dominican nuns. The Sinsinawa Dominicans accepted this advice and after years of revising the English Dominican constitutions, they received final Roman approval as a pontifical congregation in 1893. Gaining independence from the local bishop brought the Dominicans closer in structure to the Society of the Sacred Heart and the B.V.M.'s. Yet their assertion of a connection with the educational and spiritual traditions of the six-hundred-year-old Dominican order distinguished them from groups who claimed nineteenth-century foundations.

Educational Views of the Religious Orders

Given the many differences in the foundations of the four orders examined in this study, they might be expected to hold varied attitudes toward education. Yet these women were united by a common lifestyle and religious belief which transcended dissimilarities. All four orders believed that religion should form the core of women's education.

From its earliest years, the Society of the Sacred Heart clearly stated the reason for its existence. According to the 1805 Plan of the Institute, the order was to glorify the Sacred Heart by laboring for the salvation and perfection of its members as well as others.[27] In her old age, Madeleine Sophie Barat recalled the original purpose for the founding of the Society.

> The first idea we had of the form to be given to our Society was to gather the greatest number possible of true adorers of the eucharistic Heart of Jesus. . . .
>
> And so I came to the primordial idea of our little Society of the Sacred Heart: to gather together young girls to establish a community which night and day would adore the Heart of Jesus outraged in his eucharistic love. But, I said to myself, when we shall be twenty-four religious able to replace each other on the priedieu to keep up perpetual adoration, that will be much but very little for so noble an end. But if we had pupils whom we could form to the spirit of adoration and of reparation, that would be different.
>
> And I saw those hundreds, those thousands of adorers before a universal monstrance, lifted above the Church. That is it, I said to myself before a lonely tabernacle, we must vow ourselves to the education of youth.[28]

With this hope of gathering thousands of true adorers of the Sacred Heart, Barat and her companions opened their first school at Amiens in 1801. They developed a feminine version of the Jesuit *Ratio Studiorum* in 1805 and followed the usual pattern of feminine education, which included "religious instruction, moral formation, domestic training, social accomplishments, intellectual enjoyments, and mental disciplines."[29] The 1820 Plan offered the following subjects for four intermediate classes: Christian doctrine, the New Testament, reading (French and Latin), writing, chronology, mythology, grammar, spelling, elements of literature, sacred and profane history, geography, arithmetic, needlework, accomplishments, domestic economy, and habits of order. In 1852 natural history and modern languages were added as well as a superior class that studied philosophy, ancient and modern languages, modern history, elementary physics, chemistry, poetry, and apologetics.[30] The 1852 Plan of Studies was the last one to which Barat contributed. Its opening paragraph summarized her conviction about the relationship of religion to the curriculum. Education in religion was seen as the "soul of the training which the children of the Sacred Heart receive, and it is to this science, the only one really necessary, that all other studies and activities have direct or indirect reference."[31]

None of the other religious orders designed a plan of studies for their schools, although all shared with Barat the belief that the heart of education was religious. Catherine McAuley, the founder of the Sisters of Mercy, instructed her sisters to inspire the children with a "sincere devotion to the Passion of Jesus Christ, to His Real Presence in the Most Holy Sacrament, to the Immaculate Mother of God, and to their Guardian Angels."[32] The sisters must teach the children their prayers, how to assist at Mass and prepare for confession and the other sacraments. No mention of secular instruction appeared in the rule. In "Spirit of the Institute," a document reflecting her educational philosophy, McAuley wrote that Albertus Magnus, Thomas Aquinas, and Bonaventure learned not from books but from prayer and piety. She told a story of Thomas Aquinas's visit to Bonaventure: when the Dominican asked the Franciscan to show him the books he used for his studies, Bonaventure led Aquinas to the oratory where he had his crucifix.

> "Behold," Father said, "all my books, and behold here (pointing to the crucifix) the chief book from which I derive all I teach and write. It is by casting myself at the feet of Christ crucified and supplicating light, that I have made greater progress and gained more true knowledge than by reading any books whatsoever."[33]

McAuley's views on education were strongly influenced by her observations of the Dublin schools conducted by the Kildare Place Society. This group, founded in 1811 as the Society for the Promotion of the Education of the Poor, sought to provide schooling for the poor, without interfering with religious beliefs. Yet the Kildare Place Schools were far from being non-sectarian. Not only were they staffed by Protestant teachers but bible reading was mandatory, a provision Catholics found especially repugnant. Like other Catholics of their day, McAuley feared the effect of this Protestant education on Catholic children.

But far from advocating a system of schooling that was free of sectarian influence, McAuley sought to strengthen the bonds between education and religion. She believed that secular instruction must be linked to religion so that Catholic children would not regard religion as distinct from the rest of their lives.[34] The American Sisters of Mercy followed McAuley's advice on the schools. The 1888 Guide for the Sisters of Mercy in the United States noted that

> to labour generously in the schools is to deal in the salvation of souls by wholesale; it is the unostentacious means of preventing multitudes of sins; it is to extend the influence of religion far, far away beyond our own limited sphere; it is to become indirectly instruments in the salvation of numberless souls yet uncreated.[35]

In a commentary on her order's rules concerning the schools, a Sister of Mercy in Chicago pointed to the spiritual benefits accrued by the nuns through their teaching. She told them the least services rendered to the children during the day would be sanctified and made acceptable to God if performed with pure and supernatural motives. Otherwise, their work was lost for all eternity. The writer also reminded her colleagues of their important mission on earth.

> Whilst other religious orders endeavor by corporeal austerities to subject the flesh to the spirit, or employ themselves night and day singing the Divine praises, those instituted for the instruction of youth render the members of Jesus Christ subject to their head, and dispose souls for singing His praise eternally in heaven. How grateful you should be to God for having called you to an order, the members of which are, to some extent God's coadjutors.[36]

While the American Mercies adopted McAuley's views on the necessity of religion in education, they also stressed the importance of teaching secular subjects well. Their work among Catholics in such urban centers as Chicago convinced the Mercy nuns that providing a sound training in academic subjects was an indirect but very powerful way of attracting children to God.[37]

Terence Donaghoe, the B.V.M.'s priest-director, believed that religious instruction was the first purpose of education, but like the American Mercies, he recognized the importance of secular instruction. In the 1845 B.V.M. Rule, Donaghoe expressed his educational philosophy.

> What is the leading object of the Society? It consists in teaching young persons of their own sex in honor of the Sacred Childhood of Jesus Christ, 1st the practice of every virtue, 2nd the knowledge of religion and 3rd to form their hearts to the love of God. Will the parents of these children require nothing else? Yes, they do, and generally insist upon the secular instruction of their children more than the knowledge of religion which alone can make them good members of society. What are the sisters to do when parents give or appear to give the preference to secular knowledge? Sisters must, nevertheless, cherish their love to honor the Sacred Childhood of J.C., by endeavoring to possess as also to inspire their pupils with this Divine love. What then have they to do with the secular learning? The sisters sanctify their secular studies by prayer, and recommend themselves by the ability they show and the industry they use in the advancement of their pupils and thereby attract the parents and children to serve Jesus Christ which is the true way to honor his Sacred Childhood in young persons of their own sex.[38]

Mary Clarke echoed Donaghoe in the 1884 edition of *The Book of Common Observance*. She noted that the goal of her Institute was the "salvation of our souls, worked out in the salvation of our neighbor through education of youth."[39] Aware that pupils would never attach themselves to the B.V.M.'s or take pleasure in learning their religion unless they were efficient teachers, Clarke instructed the sisters on the importance of acquiring and imparting secular knowledge and keeping the schools progressive with the times.[40]

Teaching secular subjects well did not blur the real purpose of a B.V.M. education. While the nuns held themselves responsible for the physical, intellectual, and moral training of their students, their ultimate goal was the "religious training of the thousands and thousands of precious souls" committed to their charge.[41] To this end, the B.V.M.'s taught children their prayers, how to examine their conscience, prepare for confession, assist at mass, and make mental prayer. They also placed special emphasis on the fifteen mysteries of their religion, the rosary, and the way of the cross. Clarke believed that the religious instruction of the pupils would have results "favorable to their salvation," and she concluded her directions regarding the schools with the words of Jesus Christ: "He that shall go and teach, he shall be called great in the Kingdom of Heaven."[42]

Like Mary Clarke, Samuel Mazzuchelli believed that the teaching of Christian doctrine constituted the fundamental purpose of the Sinsinawa Dominicans.

> The Sisters, then, in teaching the Christian doctrine, by words and example, to the children of this country, where they are exposed to lose their faith, do fulfill the main duty of their vocation, and become the true children of their Patriarch, and worthy of the name of the Order of Preachers.[43]

He also promised heaven to his teachers.

> The Dominican Sisters, by joining the army of the Church Militant against error and sin, become active members of the militia of Jesus Christ, according to their original vocation, which is the most glorious and exalted station in human life, and well worth leaving their homes, their relatives, and all worldly affections, in the well-grounded hope of that exceedingly great reward, the eternal possession of God the Father, Son and Holy Ghost.[44]

This assurance of eternal reward and the overwhelming belief in the religious nature of education outweighed any differences that separated the orders examined in this study. It is clear from the rules and constitutions as well as the writings of the sisters that they shared the same goals in their schools and held identical hopes for their pupils.

Education of the Sisters

Because the communities viewed their mission in the schools as a spiritual one, they directed most of their energies to the religious training of their nuns. Their rules and constitutions gave specific instructions for the spiritual formation of sisters while generally ignoring intellectual development.

In practice, however, none of the orders completely neglected the intellectual training of its sisters. Many of the early members of the Society of the Sacred Heart and the Mercies entered with good educations and passed their learning on to the next generation of sisters. The Society of the Sacred Heart showed the greatest concern for the academic preparation of its recruits. In large part because of her own superior education, Madeleine Sophie Barat, the founder of the Society of the Sacred Heart, believed that religious teachers must be well trained. In addition to encouraging educated women to join her order, she made plans to open a central school for sisters who had successfully completed the period of initial formation. In 1866, the year following Barat's death, a juniorate was established, which provided teacher-training after the two-year novitiate. At the same time, the Society in America established a training school for the religious at Kenwood Academy of the Sacred Heart in Albany, New York.[45] Because of lack of funds and demands on personnel, the other orders did not follow the example set by the Society of the Sacred Heart. Most of the education received by the Mercies, B.V.M.'s, and Sinsinawa Dominicans took place during the novitiate. But this was generally inadequate because the largest portion of time was spent in spiritual occupations and menial labor.[46]

The problems of schooling the sisters were compounded when the original members possessed little formal education. Mary Frances Clarke, the B.V.M. founder, recognized the limitations of her early recruits and she required them to study one hour each day. In addition, she expected her nuns to pay special attention to their preparation of lessons and recitations in the classroom. Because the demand for teachers was so strong, the B.V.M.'s resorted to in-service teacher-training. For a while, Clarke stopped assigning young nuns to the classroom until they had completed their novitiate. But she soon changed her mind about keeping postulants and novices at the motherhouse for more than two years since few educational stimuli and cultural opportunities were available to the sisters. Moreover, the rural life at the B.V.M. motherhouse was rigorous and a number of early recruits died from the effects of hard physical labor. For these reasons, Clarke finally decided that her new members should spend one year at the motherhouse and one year on mission.[47]

The early Sinsinawa Dominicans also shared these problems with the B.V.M.'s. Like Clarke, Samuel Mazzuchelli paid special attention to the education of his sisters. In the evenings he instructed them in scripture, literature, history, sciences, and Italian. He also required them to attend his weekly lectures to the girls in the academy. Although the order in its early years gained a few well-educated recruits who helped upgrade the community intellectually, most Dominicans received their teacher-training on the job. Like the B.V.M.'s and the Mercies, the Sinsinawa Dominicans also sent out their novices and postulants to teach in the schools with very little preparation. Indeed, this remained a common practice well into the 1920s.[48]

Only when dioceses and states began demanding teacher certification at the turn of the nineteenth century did religious orders finally take a serious interest in the education of their members.[49] Emily Power, mother general of the Sinsinawa Dominicans, spoke for most female religious communities when she wrote her sisters in 1903 to inform them that examinations, certificates, and diplomas would be required by diocesan boards of examiners throughout the country and that it would be necessary to prepare well for them. "Each religious should realize fully and deeply that her time should be used for her community. The day is not far distant when every inefficient and indifferent teacher will be shut out from school work."[50] To prepare for this eventuality, convents and motherhouses began offering lectures and summer institutes for their sisters. In the summer of 1895, Dr. Thomas Shields, a Catholic University professor, began to give lectures at Sinsinawa and continued there for many years. Maurice Francis Egan, a famous American Catholic essayist, joined him in 1896. The Jesuits conducted an eight-day teacher institute for the B.V.M.'s in Chicago in April of

40

1898 and repeated it in Dubuque during the summer.[51] However, none of the religious orders collaborated or pooled their educational resources. Typical of the insularity of female religious orders was a 1905 circular, issued by the B.V.M. mother general, that forbade her sisters from going to public places for instruction or receiving help from anyone but a B.V.M.[52]

Although female religious orders often took an overly cautious attitude toward the education of their sisters, they were seriously handicapped by the refusal of Catholic universities to admit women.[53] In addition, many bishops denied the sisters permission to enroll in secular schools. However, the Sinsinawa Dominicans and the Sisters of Mercy managed to send a few of their members to non-Catholic universities. A Sinsinawa Dominican enrolled at the University of Wisconsin in 1904, and she was joined by nine colleagues three years later. Five Sisters of Mercy received B.A.'s and two gained M.A.'s at the University of Chicago in the first decade of the twentieth century. Yet, large numbers of sisters only started attending college after the Catholic University of America, Washington, D.C., established a summer school for sisters in 1911, and other Catholic universities throughout the country opened their doors to women. The Sinsinawa Dominicans, the B.V.M.'s and the Sisters of Mercy immediately sent a few of their members to Catholic University's Sisters College as well as to other Catholic schools, such as, Loyola of Chicago, De Paul, Marquette, St. Louis and Creighton. Six of the twenty-eight nuns enrolled in Catholic University's first summer session were B.V.M.'s, while the Sinsinawa Dominicans and the Mercies sent two of their members to this teacher-training program.[54] Although the number of sisters allowed to study full-time was very small, many nuns resented the removal of teachers from the schools and the financial burden of sending sisters to universities. Typical of the costs to a religious community were those assumed by the B.V.M.'s when six of their sisters went to Catholic University in 1911. Along with leaving six classrooms empty, the educational expenses of the sisters were six thousand dollars. This equalled the earnings of thirty sisters for one year.[55]

Ironically, the order which had the greatest financial resources and in the past had given its members the best teacher preparation now fell behind the Sinsinawa Dominicans, the Mercies, and the B.V.M.'s in securing degrees. Because their rule of enclosure required confinement to the convent and grounds, Religious of the Sacred Heart were prohibited from attending institutions of higher learning. Janet Erskine Stuart, R.S.C.J. recognized the problems arising from confinement to the resources of the convent and lack of university training. Stuart recommended that they thoroughly read the classics found in the convent's library. She also admonished the sisters to recognize their duty to educate themselves.

> Why do so many people think nuns foolish and incomplete things? Because they so often are! And why are they? Because they chose to let themselves be so. They stunt themselves by not thinking it is worthwhile to exert themselves when not obliged to. Material devotedness never fails us, thank God, but how rare is the devotedness that will brace up its powers, say only the power of expression, and labor and chisel and polish until it is excellent. So we remain, a great many of us, in a rut of material devotedness, and leave mental devotedness to the few who are willing for it. There ought to be so many of us who are excellent, and there are but few.[56]

Not until the early 1920s did the Society of the Sacred Heart send its sisters to universities, nearly a decade after the first group of women religious had matriculated.[57]

Although many sisters received college degrees, only a few obtained them in four years or less. Most nuns were still sent out to teach directly after the novitiate, if not before, and they attended college after school hours and during the summer.[58] As a result, it was not uncommon for a sister to take twenty years or more to obtain her degree. For a number of communities, this practice continued until the 1960s. In many instances, religious communities opened houses and began schools without adequately trained sisters to staff them. The desire to increase in number, to have many houses and to forestall others in a choice geographical area often took precedence over the academic preparation of the sisters.[59] However, the intelligence, good will and lifetime dedication to a common enterprise enabled some nuns to overcome their educational weaknesses and become excellent teachers. Unfortunately, not all teaching sisters were so gifted.

Because the communities placed so much emphasis on their religious role in the schools they could easily justify their intellectual deficiencies or simply refuse to admit them.[60] Piety took the place of secular knowledge for many sisters. Only when dioceses and states demanded certification did the orders finally recognize the necessity of acquiring training other than spiritual.

Conclusion

Despite differences in origin, history, and membership, the orders examined in this study shared the same religious goals in educating girls. Their members also led very similar lives. The women religious considered themselves to be "God's coadjutors" in the incomparable task of saving themselves and their students. They renounced families, worldly pleasures, the possibility of having a husband and children, and subjected themselves to strict vows, regulations governing every aspect of their lives, and mortification of all their senses. The nuns emphasized virginity, extreme piety, obedience, and suffering, values foreign to secular society. Yet their passionate dedication attracted thousands to their ranks.

The sisters' spirituality, training, lifestyle, and goals deeply affected the way they taught young women. Academy life reflected the world of the convent instead of that of the family or the workplace. George Sand (1804-1876), a French writer who attended a convent school in her native country, recognized what distinguished education in a convent school. Her observations are quite applicable to American academies. She wrote that nuns have far different concerns for the children under their care than anyone else. The sisters "think of nothing but heaven and hell, and for them the girl's future is her soul's salvation."[61]

Convent-School Life 3

Introduction

Convent schools gave the nuns a unique opportunity to put their spiritual ideals into practice. The sisters decided upon the intellectual, religious, emotional, and social formation that would best help their students gain entrance to heaven. Unless a girl possessed the knowledge, manners, dress, and piety proper to Roman Catholic womanhood, her soul was endangered. A 1904 catalogue from a Sinsinawa Dominican academy in Madison, Wisconsin expressed this belief and emphasized the role of the nuns: "to instill into the minds and hearts of their students those high principles of morality and religion which make virtue and refinement proof against the vicissitudes of life."[1]

The making of a Catholic gentlewoman meant injecting religion into every aspect of convent school life. This included the curriculum, schedules, rules, student organizations, and recreation. It also entailed deciding what future roles a convent school girl might choose without harming her prospect for heaven. All these decisions conformed to the values and lifestyle of the sisters who made them. This chapter explores the convent school world and the success or failure of the sisters in shaping that world according to convent values.

The academies under study were located in or near cities and large towns. The Society of the Sacred Heart maintained City House (1827) and Maryville (1872) in St. Louis; an academy in Clifton (1869), a suburb of Cincinnati; and the Taylor Street Academy (1858) in Chicago, which relocated in suburban Lake Forest in 1904. The B.V.M.'s administered in Dubuque, Iowa: St. Joseph Academy (1843) and Mt. St. Joseph (1881); and in Davenport, Iowa: Immaculate Conception Academy (1844). St. Clara Academy (1852) in Sinsinawa, eight miles east of Dubuque, and Sacred Heart Academy (1871) in Madison, Wisconsin, were Sinsinawa Dominican schools. St. Xavier Academy (1846) in Chicago was staffed by the Sisters of Mercy. Other institutions, which are mentioned in less detailed fashion, include the B.V.M. schools in Council Bluffs, Iowa and Wichita, Kansas; the Sacred Heart academy in St. Joseph, Missouri, and the Mercy academy of St. Agatha in Chicago.

Enrollment in these convent academies was generally between one and two hundred girls. Although the girls at the academies ranged in age from six to twenty-two, most were teenagers. The sisters admitted the very young only if they were orphans or children of a widowed father or sick mother. Most of the girls came from the town or the city in which the school was located. The rest came from neighboring areas while only a small percentage lived more than a day's trip from the school.[2]

Many parents sent their daughters to the convent school for First Communion preparation. Because most pupils spent only a year or two at the academy, the nuns concentrated on giving the girls a very strong religious training. The instructions to the teachers of Christian doctrine at the Academy of the Sacred Heart in Maryville in 1917 made this clear. "All the chief points necessary for salvation should be taught each year in a manner suited to the age of the students, so that if they leave after that year, they will know enough to save their souls."[3]

Since all the academies charged a substantial fee for

tuition and room and board, the girls necessarily came from well-to-do families. The costs at St. Clara in 1867 were $175 per year in addition to $36 for the piano, $80 for the harp, $24 for drawing, $36 for painting, and $20 for either Latin, French, German, or Italian. By 1909 tuition rose to $250 for the academy, with added fees for piano, violin, pipe organ, voice, and painting. Likewise, the B.V.M. academy in Dubuque, Mt. St. Joseph, charged $150 in 1887 and $240 in 1909, plus extras. [4]

Tuition and fees were higher at the Mercy and Sacred Heart academies than at the B.V.M. or Dominican schools. At St. Xavier in Chicago, the tuition reached $300 per year in 1877, though it dropped to $250 in 1899. Extras included $60 for the piano, violin, banjo, and zither; and $80 for the harp, violin, and oil painting. The Sacred Heart Academy in Clifton charged $200 in 1870 and $250 in 1899. Maryville cost $300 in 1900 and $350 in 1916. Prices for extras included $120 for vocal training, $100 for violin and harp, $80 for piano, $60 for oil painting, and $40 for drawing. [5]

Student financial accounts gave a more detailed picture of the costs of an academy education. From February 1871 to September 1872, the bill for two sisters at the Clifton academy totaled $1,255.16. This included room, board, tuition, music and instrumental lessons, books and fees for the summer months. [6]

Payment of fees was not always prompt and occasionally not forthcoming. Some parents cancelled their debts in unusual ways, such as the St. Louis families who during the 1860s paid in lambswool and potatoes. [7] A few students attended the academies without paying. In 1886 three out of twenty-seven girls at City House in St. Louis were gratis pupils. [8] These students sometimes found it difficult to be the recipients of the sisters' charity. As one St. Clara girl explained in an 1898 letter, she had found great happiness at Sinsinawa despite the fact that the nuns constantly reminded her of her status as a free pupil. Although she had been careful not to appear ungrateful, this schoolgirl noted that she did not "feel obliged to apply as a dishwasher in a kitchen full of postulants." [9]

Most of the girls were between twelve and seventeen years of age. They came from a city or large town where the school was located, stayed at the academy for one to two years and associated with girls from comfortable backgrounds. They would become part of the small but influential American Catholic middle class.

Academic Life

When designing the curriculum of the academy, the nuns kept in mind the true purpose of education. It was, as a teacher at St. Clara explained,

> . . . above all, if sound and true, at all times, in every place, and under every condition, a nearer approach of mind and soul to God. The aim of one's education should be identical with one's aim in life which is primarily God and His glory.[10]

Naturally, religion formed the core of the curriculum and was brought to bear on the other courses whenever possible.

At mid-century the convent schools offered a large number of subjects. Immaculate Conception Academy in Davenport in 1858 typified the convent-school curriculum.

> Orthography, Reading, Writing, Arithmetic, Grammar, Composition, Elocution, Geography (ancient and modern), History (sacred and profane), Algebra, Book-keeping, Astronomy, with the use of Globes, Mythology, Rhetoric, Chemistry, Natural Philosophy, Physiology, Botany, the French and German languages, Music on the Piano, Guitar, etc., Drawing in Crayon, Monochromatic and Polychromatic; also, Grecian and Oriental Painting, and practical instruction in Needle-work, both plain and Ornamental.[11]

During the 1860s and 1870s, the academies trimmed the number of subjects taught and established graded curriculums for their primary and secondary divisions. While these changes brought the academies into line with American public schools, the disproportionate emphasis on religion left its mark.[12] Indeed, although the sisters improved their academies throughout the nineteenth century, they failed to match the education given in reputable non-Catholic girls' schools

and public high schools.[13] The sisters' lack of formal education made it difficult for them to offer a first-rate academic
schooling until the twentieth century.

The following section describes the convent academy
curriculum for secondary students and the changes which
occurred in some of the courses offered.

Religion

Because the primary aim of Catholic schools was a religious one, the study of religion held first place in the curriculum. The Society of the Sacred Heart spoke for all the religious orders when it described religion in its constitutions as
the "foundation and the crowning point of the education
they intend to give, and consequently the chief subject
taught; the rest is only accessory, yet necessary in its degree."[14] In their religion courses the sisters emphasized
Christian doctrine, bible history, church history, the bible,
and philosophy.

The girls learned Christian doctrine through the study
and memorization of the catechism. As late as 1917, students
at Maryville were expected to master the following material
from various catechisms.

> The Little Catechism (Baltimore) should be reviewed in each Divi-
> sion of Christian doctrine every year, as well as three questions
> given daily in every English Class.
>
> First Division—Wilmer's Handbook of the Christian Religion.
>   Three Years' Course.
> Year A—Faith and the Creed.
>   Apologetics: Divine Origin of Christian Revelation.
>   (c. III. Art. I.) Constitution and Marks of the Church.
>   Infallibility.
> Year B—Hope, Grace, Prayer and the Sacraments.
>   Apologetics: Part I. Section II. The Church.
> Year C—Charity. Basis of Morality, Commandments and Chris-
>   tian Perfection. (The obligations and prohibitions of
>   each Commandment supplemented.)
>
> A review should be made each year of the chief points of Catho-
> lic doctrine, obligation, etc., necessary to save one's soul.

Second Division—Deharbe's Complete Catechism, No. 1.
(Schwartz, K. & F.)
All the chief points necessary for salvation should be taught
each year in a manner suited to the age of the students, so that
if they leave after that year, they will know enough to save their
souls. One portion is stressed each year as follows:
Year A—Faith and the Creed.
Year B—Hope and the Means of Grace.
Year C—Charity and the Commandments.

Third Division—Deharbe's Catechism, No. 2 (Schwartz, K. & F.)
A review should be made each year of the chief points of Catholic doctrine, obligation, devotions.

Fourth Division—Baltimore Catechism, No. 2. Complete. Catholic
Devotions: Holy Sacrifice of the Mass (Vestments, Sacred Ves-
sels, etc.), Mysteries of the Rosary, Stations, etc.[15]

The pupils memorized answers to almost every conceivable
question about God, the church, and salvation. In an 1891
examination at St. Xavier Academy one girl discussed the
four marks of the church. She knew that the church was one
because in all times and places it possessed the same faith,
sacraments, and one common head; holy because the
founder was holy; Catholic because the church had existed in
all ages, taught all nations, and maintained all truths; and
apostolic because it could trace its origin to the Apostles, a
claim no other Christian religion could make because they
had all arrived "1500 years too late to be Apostolic."[16] When
asked a similar question in 1893, a St. Clara girl answered
that the church had never altered or corrupted the apostolic
tradition because the writings of the fathers showed the
church to have been the same as it was in the present time.[17]
Other questions tested the girls' knowledge of the nature of
God. Students were asked to explain the creator's infinite
mercy, wisdom, and amicability, and why God allowed persecutions and human suffering. Teenage girls also discussed
the impossibility of denying divine revelation and proved
that the mysteries were not contrary to reason.[18]

Along with Christian doctrine, the academies taught
church history, bible history, and the bible. Church history
was often combined with general history, despite the fact

that heresies and persecutions were also studied in religion classes. Bible history outlined the major events of the Old Testament while bible classes studied selected parts of the Old and New Testaments. The girls also learned in these classes how to reply to Protestant charges that the church kept the scriptures from the laity.[19]

Philosophy classes provided additional religious training for convent academy students. In the 1890s, Mt. St. Joseph, St. Clara, and St. Xavier began requiring philosophy and logic for third and fourth year students. As in other areas of academic endeavor, Sacred Heart academies took the lead in promoting the study of philosophy. In their first schools, the Society of the Sacred Heart taught their girls logic, psychology, ontology, and ethics. Janet Erskine Stuart, one of the Society's greatest educators, explained in 1911 that philosophy belonged in every well-grounded Catholic education "to balance on the one hand the unthinking impulse of living for the day, which asks no questions so long as the 'fun' holds out, and on the other to meet the urgency of problems which press upon the minds of the more thoughtful as they grow up."[20] Philosophy examinations given to the graduating class in all the Midwestern academies during the 1910s reflected the Society's commitment to this ideal. Students were asked to: prove the immortality of the soul from the moral law; discuss what philosophical principles had been violated by modern governments with regard to the education of children, the marriage contract, and the secularization of church property; state truths opposed to the central errors of Stoicism, utilitarianism, agnosticism, independent morality, rationalism, Cartesianism; and explain why socialism violated the dignity of the individual, the sacredness of the family, the safety of the state, the last end of man.[21]

Religion classes drilled the girls in the essentials of the Catholic faith. They memorized the catechism, studied the bible, and learned the history of the church. In philosophy courses they learned how to refute the errors of modern thought and how to apply Catholicism to every part of academic life. No subject could rival the one that was designed to teach all that was necessary for salvation.

English

English held the second place of honor in the academy curriculum and was required in every grade. The courses included composition, reading, literature, rhetoric, orthography, penmanship, and grammar. Through these lessons the nuns hoped to develop in their girls a taste for "good" literature and the ability to write and speak well.

The sisters carefully chose the literary works assigned to their pupils for class as well as the books allowed in the library. When a provincial superior of the Society of the Sacred Heart visited the academy of the Sacred Heart in Chicago in 1874, she commented on the reading of the pupils.

A passion for fiction reading is too easily developed and experience shows how fatal the consequences too frequently are. The imagination becoming unduly excited, piety is rendered distasteful, serious occupations seem intolerable, and even worse risks are often incurred. Works of Science, History and Travel by Protestant authors should be allowed with extreme caution. In the first, irreligious theories are not infrequently broached, in the second, the doctrines, discipline and usages of the Church are misrepresented and made the subject of open or covert attack; in the third, the places and things dear to every Catholic heart are turned into ridicule and contempt. All this cannot fail to make dangerous impressions on young susceptible minds.[22]

Along with selecting works that would not endanger the faith of the students, the nuns chose books for the purposes of encouraging morality, modesty, and good manners. According to the Society of the Sacred Heart's 1904 Plan of Studies, "Literature should always tend towards some practical end and be made a powerful factor in moral and Christian education. The children's future must be borne in mind and the real and serious side of life brought before them."[23] Catholic authors were favored, but non-Catholics who met the standards of the nuns were also chosen. The sisters liked the classics of English literature but shunned modern works with the exceptions of such authors as Cardinals John Henry Newman and Nicholas Wiseman.

A Sinsinawa Dominican academy in Madison offered the usual literary selections in its 1899 English classes. First year pupils read Thomas Babington Macaulay's essay on Warren Hastings, James Russell Lowell's *The Vision of Sir Launfal*, and Henry Wadsworth Longfellow's *Evangeline*. In the second year the girls studied John Henry Newman's "A Dream of Gerontius," Alfred Lord Tennyson's *The Idylls of the King*, Washington Irving's *Sketch Book*, and Macaulay's essays on John Milton and Joseph Addison. Chaucer's Prologue to *The Canterbury Tales*, Shakespeare's *Merchant of Venice* and *As You Like It*, Milton's "L'Allegro," "Il Penserosa," and "Lycidas," and Tennyson's *In Memoriam* were required of third year pupils. In the fourth year, the girls read Alexander Pope's translation of the *Iliad*, Roger de Coverly's papers in Joseph Addison and Richard Steele's *The Spectator*, Oliver Goldsmith's *The Vicar of Wakefield*, Thomas De Quincey's *Revolt of the Tartars*, Sir Walter Scott's *Ivanhoe*, James Fenimore Cooper's *The Last of the Mohicans*, Milton's *Paradise Lost* (Books I and II), and Shakespeare's *Macbeth*.[24]

Other literary selections commonly assigned in the academies included: Samuel Taylor Coleridge's *The Rime of the Ancient Mariner*, Charles Dickens's *A Tale of Two Cities*, Dante's *The Divine Comedy*, Goldsmith's *The Deserted Village*, Wiseman's *Fabiola*, Shakespeare's *Hamlet*, *King Lear*, and his historical plays.

Examinations in literature both tested the students' knowledge of the literature they read as well as their ability to integrate this material with their religion. In 1884 St. Clara girls analyzed the works of Goldsmith and Addison; Burns and Moore; Dickens and Thackeray; Whittier, Longfellow, and Lowell.[25] In the early twentieth century, the Midwestern vicariate tests of the Society of the Sacred Heart included questions on Milton, Shakespeare, Hawthorne, Goldsmith, Dante, Chaucer, Petrarch, St. Theresa, Cervantes, Bacon, and Bossuet.[26]

The sisters taught the girls how to write by assigning compositions or essays on topics of an edifying nature. Typical of these essays was that of the St. Xavier pupil who in 1891 described her encounter with a poor girl who begged for money. The student asked herself how she would feel if she had not given alms to the girl.

Would I have felt happy when I thought that a poor child might have enjoyed a little pleasure with the money that I could so easily have dispensed with. No, indeed, for besides resisting the opportunity of doing good and thereby gaining an increase of grace, I would also have an uneasy conscience, and, no matter where I would be, in a ball room or in my room that pitiful gaze of the little child would be ever before me until, I would cry aloud and in my anguish and despair, "Oh, why did I resist that golden opportunity."[27]

The Xavier pupil knew that her resolve to be charitable would never waver because the voice of God's angel would "sound clear amidst the turmoil of conscience" and prevent her from missing an opportunity to do good. Sacred Heart girls also wrote on moralistic and uplifting topics for their composition classes. In 1907 they were asked to comment on Newman's statement that great things are done by devotion to one idea; Dante's "Songs of Purgatory," and the true nature and force of evil to which Macbeth succumbed. A few years later the girls discussed the ideal of friendship in Cicero, Bacon, and Thomas à Kempis, and compared Raphael's *Sistine Madonna* to St. Bernard's *Prayer to the Virgin in Paradise*.[28]

English classes in the convent school combined academic training with the inculcation of religious and moral ideals. The sisters' choice of reading material and writing assignments gave them the chance to mold the students' minds in ways consonant with Roman Catholicism and the convent.

History

The study of history, like English, was used to reinforce religious lessons. The nuns in the academies presented the Catholic version of the past and tried to connect all important events of each period with the history of the church. Madeleine Sophie Barat, founder of the Society of the Sacred Heart, also thought that this subject could draw the students closer to God.

Let us put history into their souls; without that, memories will fade and we shall have wasted our time. In seeing the empires

54

that rise and fall one after the other, they will perhaps learn to rise above their own troubles. They will thus better understand the "sic transit gloria mundi," and their hearts, disillusioned with what is nothing, will be more strongly drawn to Him who alone remains in the midst of so many ruins.[29]

The academies of the Sacred Heart taught history in every grade while the other schools only offered it during two of the four years of high school. Sacred Heart girls learned ancient, medieval, English, modern, and American history. The other academies taught ancient, general or modern, and American history. Beginning in the first decade of the twentieth century, the history of Greece and Rome replaced ancient history in the curriculum at St. Clara, Mt. St. Joseph, and St. Xavier. This coincided with the introduction of a classical program designed to prepare the girls for college.

Examinations given at the academies indicated how the nuns taught history and for what purpose. In an 1884 test at St. Clara, the girls discussed the battle between Christian heroes and Mahometon rulers. A few years later, the sisters asked how literature, philosophy, art, and science should be judged and whether a nation could be called civilized whose physical development exceeded its intellectual and whose intellectuals excluded duty to God.[30] The strongest Catholic interpretation of the past occurred in the Sacred Heart academies as shown in their examinations. A 1909 test asked the students to judge by ethical principles: the deposition and execution of Charles I; the Spanish Inquisition; the suppression of the Jesuits; the policies of Richelieu; and the revocation of the Edict of Nantes. The girls were asked to discuss the statement that the national prosperity and literary achievement of the northern nations was caused by Protestantism. They also were required to explain how the medieval papacy saved Europe from anarchy and why the Inquisition was a lawful means to an end.[31]

History in the academies provided the girls with a knowledge of the past which would reinforce their religious beliefs. The students learned about the church's vital importance in every historical period and its unblemished record from its inception to the present.

Languages

Although secular colleges and universities required Latin and Greek for admission, convent academies made no provision for instruction in these languages until the turn of the century.[32] Indeed, until the 1890s, only the academies of the Sacred Heart required the study of a foreign language. The other academies offered languages, but students were compelled to pay an extra fee. During the nineteenth century all convent academies taught French, while Latin, Greek, German, Italian or Spanish appeared at various times in the different schools.[33]

In their language classes the academies assigned the same material. Third and fourth year students of Latin read Cicero and Virgil while Greek pupils translated St. John's Gospel and Homer. Those in French classes studied Racine, Moliére, Madame de Sévigne, and Fénelon's *Telemaque*.[34] Because French formed an integral part of the Sacred Heart curriculum and was required for conversation during breakfast and when addressing the nuns, more was required of the Sacred Heart girls. In addition to what the other pupils read, the Sacred Heart schools added Lamartine, Chateaubriand, Pascal, Bossuet, Madame de Maintenon, and la Fontaine.[35]

Like English, the study of languages allowed the sisters to choose reading material that suited their religious and moral convictions. The nuns also made decisions about the pupils' future by deciding whether to offer languages needed for university admission. Until the turn of the century, the sisters regarded the classical languages as unsuitable for the feminine mind and therefore failed to prepare the girls for education beyond the academy. The inclusion of these languages in the academies signalled an acceptance by the nuns of the possibility of Catholic women gaining a higher education. Ironically, by the time most of the academies in this study incorporated Latin and Greek into their curriculums, these languages were no longer required for university admission.[36]

Mathematics and Science

Because mathematics and the other sciences afforded the nuns few opportunities to teach religion or inculcate morality, they placed little emphasis on these subjects. Still, convent academies offered classes in practical and higher arithmetic, algebra, plane and solid geometry as well as botany, astronomy, physiology, geology, chemistry, and physics. The girls were required to take the same mathematics classes throughout the period while the number of sciences studied was reduced in the second half of the period under study. From 1860 to 1890, the girls would often study three or four sciences in the same school year which made instruction little more than rudimentary. Later, at St. Clara Academy, girls enrolled in the classical program took no sciences at all.

Most of the nuns viewed mathematics and the other sciences as masculine subjects and not proper for young ladies. Janet Erskine Stuart, a Society of the Sacred Heart educator, believed that girls possessed less aptitude for mathematics than boys and had almost no occasion to make practical use of this subject in later life. She also argued against experimental sciences taught in a laboratory because they had so "little connexion with after life."[37] Stuart's views reflected the official position of the Society of the Sacred Heart who in its 1904 Plan of Studies described the sciences as mere accessories and not worthy of the time spent on more serious subjects. Nothing more than polite acquaintance with the sciences should be required of the students.[38] Physiography, a study of the stars, eclipses and calendars proved an exception to the rule since this subject could be a "new means of filling their minds with admiration for the works of creation and of inspiring them with loving reverence for the Infinite Majesty of God."[39]

Examinations

The sisters used oral, written, and public examinations to evaluate the students in academic subjects. During the school year the girls took periodic tests and quizzes while the end of each term brought comprehensive examinations in all the other subjects.

Most frightening to the girls were the public examinations conducted by clergy and laymen. In 1884 Professor Orestes Brownson, son of the famous convert, orally examined the girls at St. Clara in chemistry, logic, geology, astronomy, philosophy, physical geography, and American history. Three priests evaluated their written tests in mathematics, English, history, literature, and religion.[40] Although public examinations ended by 1900 in the academies under study, written and oral tests continued to be the norm.

The Society of the Sacred Heart employed a more elaborate method of testing than the other orders. The nuns marked their students' daily classroom performance and held competitions every Friday afternoon. Results were read aloud on Monday morning and posted for one week. Oral exams in front of the school took place at the end of the term. The Society believed that fostering competition among students made them work harder. In the beginning of the twentieth century, the Society used standardized tests to examine graduating classes in history, mathematics, compositon, philosophy, Latin, French, and literature. Prepared and graded by various Religious of the Sacred Heart in different schools, these exams were rigorous and comprehensive.

Accomplishments

Outside the academic curriculum yet integral to convent school life was the extensive training given to the girls in art and music, the so-called accomplishments. In contrast to reputable non-Catholic schools, Catholic academies emphasized the fine arts.[41]

In 1867 St. Clara taught piano, harp, guitar, voice, painting, and drawing. By 1900 the fine arts program had been expanded to include the pipe organ, banjo, mandolin, violin, oil painting, china painting, water colors, and tapestry. The Sinsinawa Dominicans also established a special department called the "School of Music," with graded courses in piano, violin, and voice as well as a "School of Art." Mt. St. Joseph and St. Xavier taught almost identical subjects to St. Clara. The only variation was in St. Xavier's offering of wax work in 1873 and zither in 1899.[42]

Art and music lessons gave the sisters few opportunities to teach religion. Their value lay in providing the girls with safe hobbies which would not lead to sin. The Society of the Sacred Heart, however, took a different view than the other communities on music and art. The Religious of the Sacred Heart believed that these studies led to vanity, overexcited the imagination, and impaired the child's health. They also felt that they were forced to yield to parents who sent their children to the academy for piano and singing. "If their children play brilliantly and are able to sing difficult music, parents consider their education complete."[43] Although Sacred Heart academies included music and art in their curricula, the nuns remained convinced that precious time and solid instruction was sacrificed on their behalf. Because they could not curb the excesses of the times, the sisters consoled themselves with the belief that under the influence of the Sacred Heart "these children may learn the worthlessness of a talent acquired at so great a cost."[44] Guided by a strict and very religious Plan of Studies, the Society feared any subject which did not directly refer to God or the church. None of the other orders under study designed such a plan and were able to view music and art as integral to the making of a Catholic gentlewoman.

Practical Training

Until the end of the nineteenth century, the cultivation of musical and artistic talents, along with instruction in embroidery, sewing, and needlework, constituted the practical training offered in the convent school. These skills prepared the girls for the convent or cultured motherhood.

Although the nuns held firmly to traditional ideas about women's roles, they were forced to acknowledge that not all their pupils married or entered the convent. By the 1890s it was clear that a significant number of convent graduates supported themselves either temporarily or permanently. All the academies, except those of the Sacred Heart, began to offer commercial subjects and courses leading to a teacher's certificate as well as the languages necessary for university admission.[45] Convent schools finally began to imitate the academic standards set by reputable non-Catholic secondary schools.

Only the academies of the Sacred Heart refused to offer vocational courses. When the superior-general, Mabel Digby, visited the United States in 1899, she disapprovingly commented on the demand of some Americans for practical training in Sacred Heart schools.[46] Following her visit, the Society more strongly emphasized its aim to train girls in Catholic culture and refinement. Not only did the Sacred Heart Religious resist external pressures to modernize their curriculum, but they remained insistent that Catholic education should prepare a girl for the home or the convent. A possible explanation for the Society's position might be that many Sacred Heart girls came from families wealthier than other academy girls and were not forced to work for a salary. In this respect, the curriculum in Sacred Heart academies would have prepared girls for their roles as Catholic gentlewomen.

Unlike the Religious of the Sacred Heart, the B.V.M.'s, Mercies, and Sinsinawa Dominicans did not address in their writings, the issue of curriculum change. Yet the addition of vocational courses indicates the sisters' awareness of new needs among the students. The change in curriculum, however, must not be confused with a change in the sisters' conception of proper feminine roles. The office worker, teacher, and university graduate could never rival the nun or the homemaker in the sisters' hierarchy for Catholic womanhood.

Criticism of the Convent School Curriculum

Before the academies changed their curriculum to include practical training and preparation for the university, many observers agreed that convent academy education did not meet the intellectual standards set by reputable secondary schools in the non-Catholic world. Most telling were the criticisms which originated from within the Catholic community. Typical of this criticism was an 1869 *Catholic World* article, which called convent academies the most respectable schools in the nation but institutions which followed educational traditions better suited to the social arrangements of

European countries. Not only did Catholic academies under-value intellectual pursuits but they overemphasized the culti-vation of affections, exterior graces, sentiments, and accom-plishments. As a result, the academies failed to provide a solid academic education.[47]

Criticism of the convent school grew stronger in the later half of the nineteenth century as women's education steadily improved. Unlike the existing convent school academies, new women's colleges such as Vassar, Smith, and Bryn Mawr, provided sound academic training and prepared its graduates for careers in the outside world. Maurice Francis Egan, a renowned Catholic writer, questioned the quality of teaching in the academy and called attention to the sad spec-tacle of the convent school graduate who left to make her way in the world with a mere smattering of accomplish-ments.[48] A former convent school girl, Katherine Tynan, dis-cussed the weaknesses of convent-school education.

> The nuns hitherto have taken education very lightly. They have gone into the convent with just so much knowledge as they re-ceived in the convent. They are forbidden newspapers, books, and reviews, almost entirely. The years advance, but they stand still. They do not realize that for women especially the world has changed, so much that a woman's personality has changed with it.[49]

In 1913, an article in the *Educational Review,* a secular publica-tion, described convent school teaching as imitative and lack-ing in originality. The writer believed that only the convent school's competition with secular schools kept it from lag-ging even farther than it did behind the times.[50]

As late as 1917, Reverend James A. Burns, a renowned American Catholic educational historian, discussed the need and demand for Catholic academies which offered more than a cultured education to their students.[51] He noted that about one-half of all convent schools aimed chiefly at a cultural education and taught no utilitarian subjects. Many Catholic girls were left without sufficient preparation for future employment.

> There is evidently a serious defect in the adjustment of education to individual and social needs, where pupils who will have to go

out and seek employment as soon as they graduate spend a large part of their time in school in the study of music and other artistic accomplishments, to the entire neglect of studies that would be of immediate help to them in securing good positions.[52]

Burns pleaded for the inclusion of a commercial course and domestic science in academies which did not offer them. He also asked that the interests of girls aspiring to a collegiate education be attended to in the academies so that they could meet college requirements.

Even the defenders of convent school education admitted the intellectual deficiencies of these institutions when they praised them for ignoring the "masculine studies" which they believed would impair the development of feminine faculties.[53] Convent school supporters thought that these institutions were true nurseries of Christian womanhood where religion and virtue were instilled in the students.

> Religion, refinement, enlightened benevolence, fine womanly traits, and fearless disregard of danger in the discharge of duty— these are the things which our girls are taught in Convent Boarding Schools, both by precept and example. They learn, besides, the ordinary modicum of history, mathematics, grammar, literature and geography; even though a few solitary islands of knowledge may float away beyond their reach.[54]

The convent schools also held this view of themselves. An 1892 article in *The Young Eagle*, a St. Clara Academy student publication, extolled the non-academic virtues of academy education. The writer began by noting that although learning of the highest order could be obtained in the convent school, the value of this schooling lay in the intangible elements of modesty and humility which accompanied the learning. It gave a girl the "force of character, the pliability of disposition, the grace of manner, the modesty of demeanor, the cultivation of the mind, the elevation of sentiment which make a woman the queen of society and the angel of the household."[55] The writer disparaged a "worldly training," which imparts "a certain masculine force and gross strength that convent pupils do not possess, and if their surroundings and associations are what they ought to be, will never need."[56] She believed that convent school training encouraged nun-like qualities, which in history, fiction, drama, and real life had made women great, noble, and womanly.

The nuns' lack of appreciation for the intellectual life stemmed from their own training which emphasized the primacy of religion over all other pursuits. In addition to deepening their own spiritual lives, the nuns sought to foster these values in their students. As a result, encouraging the development of nun-like characteristics took precedence over learning in the convent school world.

Student Life

The attempt to form cultured Catholic gentlewomen extended beyond the classroom walls. It shaped the rules, dress, recreation, student organizations, and discipline of the girls. Whether in academic or social matters, the aim of the sisters remained the same, and the values of conventual life prevailed.

Schedules and Rules

Every moment of the student's day was strictly regulated. Her daily schedule closely resembled that of the nuns who taught her. The 1873 horarium for St. Francis Xavier pupils and the 1904 Sacred Heart regime typified the school girl's day.

St. Xavier	
5:30	Rise
6:15	Morning Prayers and Mass
7:00	Breakfast, followed by Recreation
8:00	Study
9:00	Recitation
11:45	Dinner and Recreation
12:30	Study and Recitation
4:00	Luncheon and Recreation
5:00	Study
6:00	Supper, Rosary
6:15	Recreation
8:15	Night Prayers, after which all retire to their respective dormitories for the night.[57]

Sacred Heart Academies		
5:55 Rise	1:30	Needlework, Two decades of the
6:30 Morning Prayers		Rosary, Said either at the begin-
6:45 Preparation of lessons		ning or end of this exercise
7:15 Mass	3:30	Gôuter
7:45 Breakfast	4:00	Preparation
8:15 Preparation	4:30	Class
9:00 Class	6:00	Written exercises
10:30 Recreation	7:00	Religious Instruction
10:45 Preparation	7:30	Supper
11:30 Writing Lessons	8:00	Recreation
12:00 Dinner	8:30	Night prayers, Dormitories[58]
12:30 Recreation		

The schedules changed only on Sundays, feast days, retreats, or visits from church dignitaries.

Along with requiring students to follow a rigid schedule, the nuns kept the girls completely isolated and tried to shut out all outside influences. They inspected incoming and outgoing mail and packages, forbade the students to receive magazines and newspapers, checked all books before the girls could read them, and allowed the pupils to leave the school grounds only when accompanied by a sister. The academies permitted visitors one afternoon a week, for a period no longer than three hours. Family members could always visit during the appointed time while unrelated females needed authorization from parents and the school. Unless related to the girl they were visiting, males were not allowed. Mt. St. Joseph relaxed their rules in 1913 when they permitted the girls to go to Dubuque with their families on the fourth Sunday of the month.

Frequent home visits were also forbidden. During the school year the girls generally returned home for one week at either Easter or Christmas. St. Clara gave the girls an Easter vacation in 1867 but switched to Christmas in 1881. By 1900 St. Clara strongly recommended that the pupils remain at school during the entire holiday. Mt. St. Joseph allowed Dubuque residents to go home on Easter Sunday and gave all pupils a Christmas vacation after 1890. The most liberal policy was that of St. Xavier which permitted one week at Christmas and a home visit on the first Sunday of the month for Chicago residents.

The sisters closely regulated behavior in the schools. They demanded silence at all times except recreation and selected meal periods and required the girls to move in double file and in response to the signal of a teacher. A nun always supervised the girls whether in the classroom, in the dormitories, or walking about on school grounds.

Dress codes at the various academies sought to banish worldly vanity from adolescent hearts. A passage from the Sinsinawa Dominican Rule reflected this concern of the nuns.

> Nothing should be allowed the children, either in their clothing or the furniture of their apartments, which savors of the spirit of the world, but they must be formed to all virtue and modesty such as should reign in Convents and among Religious women, whose minds should be wholly turned away from secular vanities.[59]

The pupils wore modest, dark, nunlike clothing, such as the navy blue serge dress of St. Xavier girls or the gray skirt and navy blue shirtwaist of Mt. St. Joseph students. In the 1880s, Maryville required long black cashmere uniforms with black alpaca aprons and white collars. This uniform gave way to black wool skirts, with black-and-white checked gingham blouses in the next decade. Only on Sundays were academy students allowed to vary their uniform. Sacred Heart girls wore white dresses while pupils from the B.V.M., Mercy, and Sinsinawa Dominican academies wore black ones.

Discipline

The sisters exhorted the girls to abide by the rules and conform to the pattern of school life. The Religious of the Sacred Heart tried to foster good conduct and diligence through a system of rewards and prizes. Every Sunday night at assembly, the reverend mother gave public praise or reproof to each girl by presenting her with a small card or premium embossed with the words "trés bien," "bien," and "assez bien." The first signified exemplary behavior. The second meant that the pupil caused some trouble. "Assez bien" indicated bad conduct but failure to receive any card brought the most humiliation. The greatest reward for good behavior was the coveted blue ribbon. Those who wore this badge had been judged by the nuns to possess good spirit, virtue, leadership, and irreproachable conduct.

The sisters also took strong measures to enforce discipline. At Sacred Heart schools, girls who had broken the rules were required to wear black veils to chapel while the rest of their classmates wore white. Other children were confined to their dormitories or deprived of recreation. St. Xavier's sisters revoked monthly home visiting privileges for their Chicago students. The nuns rarely, if ever, used corporal punishment on any of their pupils.

When a student could not be controlled, the sisters resorted to expulsion. In 1900 St. Clara noted in its catalogue that continued inattention to studies, insubordination, and bad conduct would lead to dismissal. A few years later the school added pernicious influence and refractory behavior to its list of offenses. It is difficult to determine how many girls were expelled or asked to leave the academies. However, the student register of the Academy of the Sacred Heart in Chicago and later Lake Forest indicated the number of problem students. During the 1890s seven girls were described as undesirable out of 234 enrolled. In the next decade, seventeen undesirables and ten expulsions appeared in a listing of 558 girls, but some of these dismissals occurred because of the parent's behavior, not the child's. The Academy of the Sacred Heart expelled a nine-year-old because her Catholic mother remarried after a divorce. A Protestant child was also dismissed for the same reason in 1907.[60]

Recreation

Throughout the period the academies provided various forms of recreation for the girls. The nuns tried to fill the students' leisure time with worthwhile activities, which would reinforce lessons learned in the classroom as well as allow diversions and outlets for youthful energies. This occurred in informal and more organized recreational activities.

During school hours a period was set aside for recreation, which required the girls to sew silently, embroider, or knit while a sister read pious stories to them. After school the girls were given another period for games and amusements. When weather permitted, it was common for the pupils to take walks, garden, play croquet, and use the swings. In some of the academies the girls danced before supper. On weekends the pupils would often entertain each other with songs, impromptu theater, and music. The schools also held dances for the girls. At St. Clara's Thanksgiving Ball, the major social event of the school year, the girls wore their finest dresses and danced all evening to a band brought from Dubuque. Maryville held a "Veiled Prophets Ball" each year where the students dressed in various costumes according to a set theme. In 1905 one class chose Chaucer, another Longfellow, while a third picked ancient peoples.[61] In keeping with the conventual spirit, no boys were allowed to attend any of these functions.

On special feast days and holidays, the sisters organized amusements and treats for which the girls anxiously awaited. Sacred Heart academies called these field days "congés" and they featured such games as "cache-cache," five-in-five-out, croquet, and races. No amusement rivaled that of "cache-cache" among the Sacred Heart girls. This highly competitive game required a class to divide itself into two teams, each headed by a captain. One team hid while the other searched the grounds and the school. The first group then tried to reach the goal without being discovered. Agnes Repplier, a famous American essayist who attended a Sacred Heart Academy during the 1860s, vividly remembered the importance of this game to the students.

> So much, indeed, depended upon the leader's tactics, and so keen was our thirst for victory, that the girl who saved the day for herself and for her comrades was held in higher esteem than the girl who came out ahead in the periodical blistering of examinations.[62]

Student plays, the greatest diversion of school life, also sparked tremendous excitement among the girls. Nearly always religious, these dramas were chosen by the nuns with a view to the special needs of their students. Agnes Repplier recalled that

> their salient feature was the absence of courtship and of love. It was part of the convent system to ignore the master passion, to assume that it did not exist, to banish from our work and from our play any reference to the power that moves the world. . . . The students of St. Omer—so I have been told—presented a French version of "Romeo and Juliet," with all the love scenes left out. This tour de force was beyond our scope; but "She Stoops to Conquer," shorn of its double courtship, made a vivacious bit of comedy, and a translation of "Le Malade Imaginaire" expurgated to attenuation—was the most successful farce of the season.[63]

Expurgation was of course done by the nuns with the result that famous plays were left unrecognizable. Many of the dramatic productions staged at the academies were original works, written by one of the nuns. "They were, as a rule, tragic in character, and devout in sentiment—sometimes so exceedingly devout as to resemble religious homilies rather than legitimate drama."[64] The girls especially enjoyed historical dramas with great names and important incidents. They thrilled to the emotional and passionate renditions of the parts and idolized the stars. Male parts, however, posed a problem because the girls were not permitted to don male attire. The nuns compromised by allowing the girls who portrayed male characters to wear short skirts reaching to their knees.[65]

Standard plays in the convent school repertoire included *Joan of Arc, Thomas á Becket, The Fable of the Ugly Duckling, She Stoops to Conquer, Mary, Queen of Scots, Claudia, the Daughter of Pilate, Notre Dame of Lourdes, The Vestals,* and a Japanese martyr play.[66] All these dramas contained strong religious and moralistic messages. *The Fable of the Ugly Duckling,* written by Janet Erskine Stuart, a member of the Society of the Sacred Heart, was described in its introduction as a fable showing "how the soul, which is an Ugly Duckling, by adversity and experience, and the abhorrence of worldliness, may attain to true life."[67]

Clubs in the academies fostered interest in leisure time activities that the nuns judged suitable for cultured Catholic women. These included reading circles or literary societies, musical groups, and writing groups. Meetings were held after class hours or on the weekends.

Reading circles chose a particular book or poem from which to read aloud and later discuss. At St. Clara in 1902 there existed a Thomas Aquinas Club for the reading of Dante, Our Lady of Mt. Carmel for Shakespeare, the Mazzuchelli Reading Circle for English authors, the Rosary Circle for American writers and the St. Agnes Group for Longfellow. At Mt. St. Joseph the girls joined the Assissium Society, where they discussed their own essays, or the Alexandrian and Loras Circles which were founded for the "purposes of promoting the acquisition of independent thought and ease of expression."[68] St. Xavier's Euterpean Circle attempted to secure the blessings of wisdom, truth, beauty, and love for its members. Numerous musical societies also existed at the academies. St. Clara alone boasted five different groups in 1902. At least one society in each school was named for St. Cecilia, the virgin-martyr patron of music. These groups gave frequent concerts or recitals for their fellow students as well as parents and visitors.

Some of the academies founded clubs called Aethisian Societies to acquaint the girls with their future social roles. At Immaculate Conception Academy this club sought to promote a taste for intellectual pleasures, impart a greater ease of manner in society, and cultivate a love for refinement and courtesy. During their meetings in the academy parlors, the girls played the harp and the piano, sang, read, and engaged in polite conversations.[69]

Because writing was another acceptable pastime for Catholic gentlewomen, the academies sponsored student newspapers and magazines, which featured the girls' poetry, essays, and short stories. Much of the material in these publications was of a religious nature, although it also included news of the school, alumnae notes, and book reviews.

St. Xavier's Echo was the only student publication from the academies which seriously discussed current events. An 1891 issue covered Illinois news, the silver debate in Congress, Italy's new premier, and events in Brazil. The *Echo* also reviewed other Catholic school publications. In 1893 the paper commented that St. Clara's *The Young Eagle* was never known for its originality and it charged that although students served as editors, little of their work appeared in the magazine. A St. Xavier girl criticized an essay from the St. Clara paper as pretentious and obviously written by one of the Dominican sisters.[70] The newspaper from Maryville Academy stood out for its cleverness and humor in essays, limericks, mock interviews, and book reviews. In a 1907 issue, a schoolgirl parodied the story of Mother Hubbard's dog, using the style of Finley Peter Dunne, G. K. Chesterton, Omar Khayyám, and Walt Whitman. Dunne's Mr. Dooley was especially amusing.

> Hennessy, did ye iver hear iv that ould Mother Hubbard? Not wane iv thim sasiety ladies, moind ye, but wane of thim sensible ould wimmin what kapes a dog to watch the house and not to go a ridin' with thim in their kerriges. Well now, Hennessy, bein' a kind-hearted ould dame, iv course she wanted to give him something to ate, so begorra, she went to the cupboard. But, Hennessy, phat do ve think? That cupboard was as bare as the stores after bargain days. It must have been wone iv thim boodlers, not wantin' only to rob people, but most avim rob a pore baste.[71]

Another piece recounted an imaginary interview with Alice Roosevelt Longworth, daughter of President Theodore Roosevelt. When asked by the Maryville reporter if she still practiced with Indian clubs, Mrs. Longworth replied that she had replaced them with twenty-pound cannon balls that her father had picked up in Cuba, and then showed the reporter her plans for the gondola they would need for their winter seat in Havana. She also discussed her suggestion for a new Constitution since her father thought the present one too obscure. The reporter inquired whether the president ever thought, to which his daughter answered: "Of course he does not think. To think is a waste of brain power and we have no right to waste anything but other people's money."[72]

70

Sports

Organized sports began in the academies during the 1890s.[73] The sisters viewed them as extensions of the earlier informal games, a harmless means of channeling youthful energies, and a way to direct attention from the rigors of convent school life. In addition, the nuns believed that exercise helped keep the students healthy.

The pupils at all the academies quickly became interested in playing various sports. In 1891 *St. Xavier's Echo* exclaimed: "Tennis! tennis. This is the menu for breakfast, dinner, and supper since those nets have been set up."[74] During the 1890s the sports craze also came to Maryville, where girls played basketball and baseball with racquet bats, and to St. Clara, where pupils became enamored of baseball, tennis, and basketball. All the schools covered sports events in their student publications.

Student Responses

Attitudes Toward the Sisters

For the most part, convent school girls were happy and willing to abide by the rules and standards set by the nuns. The students had their favorites among their teachers, and many remained attached to them long after graduation. Louise Imogen Guiney (1861–1921), an American Catholic poet who attended a Sacred Heart academy from the age of eleven to seventeen, recalled how her reluctance to attend a convent school was dissolved by an energetic young sister. The nun took Guiney into an old garden with high, overgrown hedges.

> There the demon of mischief got into her worship, bless her! She was a young nun and full of life, and, leading a chase into one of the orchards to get me some early apples, she twice took the wide box hedge in a graceful leap, with my long thin legs enthusiastically following. I was but eleven and I judged everything by its capacity to jump, run and swim. She didn't know that, but she broke down, by that one flight in air, all my objections to a contemplative life.[75]

However, a few of the sisters never gained the affection of their pupils and were distastefully remembered. At Agnes

Repplier's school, the girls detested a nun called Madame Bouron for her "icy composure, a mock humility and polite phrases that carried a hidden sting."[76] When one of the teachers was transferred, the girls were very disappointed that it was not Madame Bouron.

> The consensus of opinion, as gathered that evening in the dormitory, was not unlike the old Jacobite epitaph on Frederick, Prince of Wales. Every one of us was sincerely sorry that Madame Bouron had not been summoned,—
>
> "Had it been his father,
> We had much rather;"[77]

Mischief

Along with arousing deep emotions of love or hatred, life-long devotion or resentment, the students responded to convent school life with pranks, mischief or rebellions. These were not recorded by the sisters but found their way into the memoirs or remembrances of alumnae.

Agnes Repplier, expelled from a Sacred Heart academy in Philadelphia, described her minor rebellions and subterfuges. Before a retreat, she and her friends stole the straw from the crib of the Christ child, giving them the "twofold stimulus of pillage and impiety."[78] They also enjoyed playing forbidden games such as their version of the temptation of St. Anthony. The girl playing the devil would take a flying leap over her kneeling friend who pretended to be the hermit. The most daring feat of Repplier and her associates was their successful smuggling of liquor and cigarettes onto school grounds. Drinking and smoking usually held the highest honor in the repertoire of convent school mischief.

The memoirs of Rhoda Walker Edwards, a Sacred Heart student in the late nineteenth century, mentioned numerous pranks and mischief among the students. Her younger sister took a joy ride with the bishop's carriage and horses while he visited the Religious at the academy. The nuns were aghast when they and the bishop discovered his carriage missing and saw one of their students happily drive up with his horses. This Sacred Heart alumna also remembered a student who played a prank on the superior. During an early

Christian martyr's play, the nun had publically admonished a young star for her overly dramatic performance. The pupil had her revenge when she appeared in the convent parlor dressed in the garb of a missionary nun, which had been smuggled in by a friend on visiting day. Her request to see the Reverend Mother was granted, whereupon

> . . . she told a pitiful tale of the poverty of the Orient and the rich treasure to be gathered in the harvest of souls that awaited their efforts. So convincing was she, that Mother Hogan not only offered to have a collection made for the benefit of the mission, but volunteered hospitality for the night. As Mamie was being conducted to the Cloister, either her courage failed or her conscience rebelled. She confessed the hoax. After a gentle reprimand by Mother Hogan, and a promise by Mamie that such an offense would never be repeated, she was forgiven[79]

Although this student was pardoned, a number of Edwards's other classmates were expelled.

Occasionally the girls became completely uncontrollable. This occurred at Maryville when an organ recital was given in mid-week. The unusual nature of a break in the daily routine and the wearing of Sunday white dresses and white veils excited the students. After two hours of organ music, the entire school literally struck. "Big and little, we turned from the ranks and ran, high, low, all over the house, while a trio of unmistakeable signal claps did their best."[80]

Other pranks were caused by the severity of some of the rules. For many of the girls, the prohibition against any contact with boys was the most unfair. A number of these pupils spent considerable amounts of time dreaming and plotting about ways to see or talk with members of the opposite sex. At one school, girls set an appointed time for boys from a nearby college to come to the academy and wave to the girls. Before the boys came, two academy pupils hung large squares of material out of a dormitory window and quickly returned to their classroom. When the principal saw the boys gather outside the school to wave at the fluttering handkerchiefs, she unsuccessfully searched every classroom for the girls who were missing at the time the boys arrived.[81] A more serious incident occurred at St. Clara in the beginning of the twentieth century when boys from Dubuque traveled to Sinsinawa in carriages. Nuns quickly posted themselves on every bench and patrolled the grounds. Still, a few of the girls jumped into the carriages with the boys and accepted cigarettes from them. Later, the sisters caught the girls smoking and held them incommunicado, which infuriated the rest of the school. After the threat of expulsion, the culprits made a public apology and all was forgiven.[82]

At Maryville Academy an enterprising young man gained admittance to the 1905 graduation exercises at which Archbishop John Glennon of St. Louis presided. Because the only outsiders allowed to attend this ceremony were priests, the intruder borrowed a Roman collar and entered the school with his fellow clerics. The ruse succeeded because Glennon seriously acknowledged the young "priest's" greeting though he recognized him as the fiancé of one of the graduates.[83]

Romantic Friendships

Catching a glimpse of boys in the distance failed to satisfy the romantic interests of many adolescent girls. Instead, they looked to each other to fulfill that need. These relationships became a way to transcend homesickness, total regimentation, and the sterility of an all-female institution.

All the academies prohibited these attachments which they called "particular friendships." The Society of the Sacred Heart noted in its 1904 Plan of Studies that a pupil was not allowed "to go apart from the rest, to play or talk with another, except with leave from the mistress."[84] The sisters believed that particular friendships sinned against charity and led to dangerous and unhealthy indulgences of feeling. They extended the convent's prohibition against these relationships to the academy and demanded that the girls hold the same attitudes toward friendship as the sisters.

Despite the rules against them, these forbidden friendships flourished in the academies. Some were passionate crushes of a younger girl on an older one as described by Agnes Repplier. "It was an ancient and honorable convent custom for the little girls in the 'Second Cours' to cultivate an ardent passion for certain carefully selected big girls in the 'First Cours,' to hold a court of love, and vie with one another in extravagant demonstrations of affection."[85] Repplier's infatuation with an older student prompted her to cut threads from her beloved's shawl, obtain a lock of her hair, and carve the girl's initials into her wrist. When young Louise Imogen Guiney fell in love, she fancied herself Uncas, the noble Indian in J. F. Cooper's *The Last of the Mohicans*. The girl she pursued was the Cora of her heart.

> . . . I adored the beautiful object from across the study-hall or the playground, to the best of my ability, and found falling in love and not 'slopping over,' quite an educative process! Best of all, as some would think, I did not love in vain.[86]

Romantic friendships between two girls of the same age often had to be hidden and various subterfuges employed in order to spend time together alone. The pupils at Maryville wrote about this problem in a 1906 issue of their student newspaper. "Pairs are not very plentiful in the Maryville vicinity; owing to the difficulty of cultivating them."[87] However, at St. Xavier in 1911, the yearbook included a humorous advice column to the lovelorn. It detailed the joys and pains of convent school courtship. One young lady asked the "Dear Abby" of St. Xavier for a remedy to cure her fickleness.

> From Freshman Year until now, so many have stolen my heart! Please give me a remedy. My love is ardent at the beginning, but I can't help it, it just evaporates after a little while. For instance, at the beginning of the year dark-eyed Mariucci Flirrtalotti held a big place in my heart and I couldn't help monopolizing all her dances at noon . . . . Then for a while I courted blue-eyed Tess, and now I have fallen deeply in love with "Black-eyed Dot," but she does not return enuf of my love.[88]

Another asked how she could show her appreciation of a suitor who expressed her ardent love through presents of flowers, theater tickets, and other attentions. The yearbook also recognized the inevitable end of most of these friendships.

To meet, to love and then to part
This is the sad, sad fate of a schoolgirl's heart.[89]

The romantic friendships experienced by convent schoolgirls were not peculiar to Catholic academies. Intense, affectionate friendships among women were very common and acceptable in nineteenth-century America.[90] However, the consequences of these relationships were more far reaching for Catholic girls than non-Catholics because the convent school provide no married role models or contact with males. Involvement with the opposite sex was far more mysterious to a convent schoolgirl than the doctrine of the Trinity or undeserved human suffering. Many convent schoolgirls discovered that their emotional needs could be met by females without exploring that possibility with men. Finally, the overwhelming desire to remain with one's beloved, whether fellow student or teacher, might have led others to confuse religious vocation with romantic friendship.

Conclusion

The sisters succeeded in imposing their values and lifestyles on every aspect of convent school life. Until the 1890s, the academy curriculum prepared girls for either convent life or pious, cultured motherhood, the two roles which the nuns found acceptable for Catholic gentlewomen. Most likely, the Society of the Sacred Heart was able to retain its traditional curriculum because they catered to a wealthy clientele, which did not demand practical training for their daughters. In contrast, the Mercies, the B.V.M.'s and the Sinsinawa Dominicans all modified their curriculum to include vocational training. These changes, however, did not compromise the rest of academy life. The schedules and rules followed by the girls matched those of their teachers and all recreational activities contained a religious and moralistic purpose.

Convent schools aimed to produce a Catholic gentlewoman whose intellect, behavior, pastimes and appearance would never endanger her soul. Essential to this task was the

76

development of a strong piety. The next chapter examines the place of religious practices in the academy and how they contributed to the sisters' concept of ideal Catholic woman-hood.

Piety   4

Introduction

eligious practices, devotions and ideals compli-
mented the academic and social dimensions of
the convent school world. Nuns used daily observances, religious celebrations, retreats, sodalities, religious models, and
spiritual literature to develop a piety which would keep both
students and alumnae faithful to convent school values.

Religious Observances

The sisters created a world in the convent school which
was permeated with Roman Catholic symbols, devotions,
and ideals.[1] They structured the girls' lives around religious
observances. A typical day at any of the academies began and
ended with prayer. Pupils rose to the sound of a bell, offered
themselves to God, and consecrated all their acts of the day
to him. The awakening girls listened to a brief prayer such as
"Sacred Heart of Jesus, Immaculate Heart of Mary," to which
they responded, "I give you my heart." They watched as a
sister sprinkled holy water throughout the dormitory and
while dressing, they were encouraged to remember the virtue of modesty and that the eyes of God and their guardian
angel were always upon them. Morning prayers and Mass

followed. Later, students recited the angelus and the rosary. Evening chapel and an elaborate examination of conscience relating to a schoolgirl's duties and temptations closed the day.[2]

Once a week the girls scrupulously prepared themselves for the sacrament of penance. Many brought to the confessional a list of sins to jog their memories. They confessed to a priest, then received absolution and an appropriate penance. Until the beginning of the twentieth century, when the Vatican urged frequent communion, the girls received the Eucharist every two weeks.[3] A pupil at St. Clara's in Wisconsin in 1860 remembered receiving Holy Communion monthly while the sisters took the sacrament twice a month. On the day before Communion, the mother superior gathered the students in the recreation room and helped them examine their consciences. "She would talk to us and many times we were all in tears as well as herself as she related the sufferings and goodness of God, Our Savior, Blessed Mother and many of the Saints."[4]

Crucifixes, statues, and paintings of the Blessed Virgin Mary, the Sacred Heart, various saints, and biblical scenes decorated every room and corridor in the school. The prize for academic excellence, good behavior, or victory in school games was a statue, a holy picture, a medal or a book of religious nature. Holidays and school celebrations were held on saints' days or feast days of one of the sisters. A former convent-school student described in her novel the effect of this atmosphere on a young girl's piety.

> She really did begin to live all day long in the presence of the court of heaven. God the Father and God the Holy Ghost remained awe-inspiring conceptions, Presences who could only be addressed in set words and with one's mind, as it were, properly gloved and veiled. But to Our Lady and the Holy Child and the saints she spoke as naturally as to her friends. She learnt to smooth a place on her pillow for her Guardian Angel to sit during the night, to promise St. Anthony a creed or some pennies for the poor in return for finding her lost property, to jump out of bed at the first beat of the bell to help the Holy Souls in purgatory. She learnt, too, to recognize all round her the signs of heaven on earth.[5]

80

The liturgical calendar determined the mood of the school at any given time of the year. Important in the calendar were Lent, Advent, the months of May and June, first Fridays, feasts of the Blessed Mother, various saints' days, and the feasts of the foundress or founder and the mother superior of the house. The academies marked these days and seasons with special rituals and celebrations.

During a special season or during the weeks prior to a major feast day, the girls prepared themselves by extra devotions, the learning of new hymns, and faithfulness to a practice or a virtue. The sisters used these periods to teach the girls the spirit of self-sacrifice, a quality which they believed integral to a Catholic woman's life. Referring to "making acts," Agnes Repplier explained how this virtue was cultivated.

> "Making an act" was the convent phraseology for doing without something one wanted, for stopping short on the verge of innocent gratification. . . If I ate my bread unbuttered, or drank my tea unsweetened, that was an act. It will be easily understood that the constant practice of acts deprived life of everything that made it worth living. We were so trained in this system of renunciation that it was impossible to enjoy even the very simplest pleasures that our convent table afforded. If there were anything we particularly liked, our nagging little consciences piped up with their intolerable "Make an act, make an act;" and it was only when the last mouthful was resolutely swallowed that we could feel sure we had triumphed over asceticism.[6]

At Maryville Academy in St. Louis, the girls adhered to the practices of silence and charity in preparation for the 1885 feast of the Immaculate Conception. The "perfectly faithful" were allowed to deposit lilies at the feet of Our Lady's statue. But girls who had broken the rule of silence and charity more than three times suffered a special humiliation. On the feast day, they were forced to wear black veils rather than white lace.[7] The 1904 practices at the Sacred Heart Academy in Clifton for the same feast day included silence at the five minute prayer, a passing salute to the statute of the Blessed Virgin, sitting erect, not crossing one's feet, recollection at prayer, six acts of charity, strict silence and three acts of mortification.[8]

May devotions to Mary provided the greatest color, pageantry and excitement of the school year. Maryville in 1915 chose to practice the courtesies of Mary and "noblisse oblige." During each week the girls wore a shield bearing the motto of page, esquire, knight, or baron to remind them to practice the courtly virtues.[9] Another school designated Mary as the "Star of the Sea." They set up a miniature lake in the study hall, with ships for all classes which advanced day by day toward the statue of Our Lady on the opposite shore. Girls competed in devotions for the coveted honor of crowning the Blessed Mother. The girl who conformed most to the practices of the school and who exhibited the greatest piety was chosen to crown the Virgin Mary. Often, the nuns selected the school rebel or troublemaker because she showed such immense improvement in behavior and piety. The crowning itself was planned to the smallest detail. The girls wore white dresses, flowered headpieces and each carried a single lily. Maids of honor were set apart by their blue sashes and colorful banners. They marched in procession through the school and the grounds, singing hymns and reciting litanies to Our Lady.[10] Each girl knelt before the statue of the Blessed Mother and recited aloud the prayer, "O Mary, I give thee the lily of my heart; be thou its guardian forever." She then placed the lily before the statue. As late as 1924, this practice remained unchanged.

> As they come to kneel and recite their prayer a great heap of lilies rises like a white wave that touches the feet of the Virgo Purissima. What comment can enhance the absolute clarity of that symbolic offering? They have placed the lily of their hearts in her hands to whom alone they can trust it with perfect surety.[11]

To offer satisfaction and reparation for the many sins of humankind, the sisters encouraged devotion to the Sacred Heart on the first Friday of every month and during the month of June. First Fridays were very special to the students attending the Academy of the Sacred Heart in Chicago at the end of the nineteenth century. During the general assembly held on this day, pupils with the two highest averages received holy pictures or medals, which according to a former student "meant more to us than millions."[12] In 1920 the Sacred Heart Academy in Clifton observed first Friday by distributing Sacred Heart badges before Mass and collecting them after breakfast. The children burned vigil lights at the shrine and recited devotions to the Sacred Heart in the study hall. An elaborate benediction with banners and guards of honor closed the day.[13]

During June, the month of the Sacred Heart, the girls prodded themselves to extra feats of self-denial. One school divided itself into bands of adorers, repairers, and expiators who changed places daily. Adorers attended a short "holy hour." Repairers knelt around the altar reciting acts of atonement. Expiators made five acts of mortification.[14]

The most solemn time of the year was the season of Lent. For forty days the girls struggled to make sacrifices which would remind them of Jesus Christ's sufferings and prepare them for Easter. The liturgical ceremonies deeply impressed some of the pupils. One former convent schoolgirl remembered the somber "Tenabrae" during Holy Week with its "lugubrious chanting of the lamentations while slowly, but inexorably, the candles were extinguished, leaving the world in darkness." Her sadness deepened on Holy Thursday when the altar was stripped and the tabernacle door left open. Relief came on Holy Saturday when bells rang again and girls sang with all their hearts, "Regina Coeli Laetare Alleluia."[15]

Whether the season was Lent or the day an ordinary one, the sisters succeeded in investing it with a religious significance. They used devotions and symbols familiar to other American Catholics but in a way that touched every part of a pupil's life. Like their teachers, convent schoolgirls lived in a world infused with religion and knew the importance of sacrificing themselves whenever possible for the sake of that religion.

Retreat

To supplement daily mass, prayers, feast days, and pious practices, a concentrated period of time was set aside each year for a more intense spiritual experience. Three to

five day retreats, usually given by a Jesuit, required strict
silence and a total devotion to religious matters. The girls
prayed, listened to sermons, attended religious services,
took meditative walks, and read spiritual works. A typical
schedule for retreat days was followed by the Sacred Heart
Academy in Clifton in 1902:

6:30	Rise	1:35	Way of the Cross
7:15	Mass	2:00	Free Time
8:15	Walk	3:00	Instruction
8:30	Free Time (Reflection)	3:30	Walk
9:00	Instruction	4:00	Free Time
10:00	Free Time	5:00	Benediction and Instruction
11:00	Spiritual Reading	6:30	Supper
12:00	Dinner	7:00	Singing Hymns
12:30	Walk	7:30	Night Prayers and Instruction[16]
1:00	Free Time		

Many girls looked forward to their retreats and convent
school annalists commented on the silence and reverence of
the students. A St. Clara girl wrote excitedly to her mother in
1897 about her upcoming retreat: "I am going to keep silence
perfectly." She later described a wonderful retreat and the
strong impression that the Jesuit director had made upon
her.[17]

During the retreat the girls listened to sermons on
death, judgment, hell, and heaven. They trembled hearing
the priest denounce pride, worldliness, infidelity, and
"many dreadful sins we stood in no immediate danger of
committing."[18] Especially terrifying was the vision of hell:

> Body and soul were to be tormented for ever and ever, with no
> interruption of agony, no numbness of habit, no ray of hope.
> Every sense would be revolted by filth and stench and noise;
> every nerve exquisitely tortured by fire to which mere earthly fire
> was as cool as water. The damned suffered always from appalling
> thirst, their swollen tongues were parched and cracked. They
> were hungry and the devils in mockery offered them white-hot
> coals to eat. They suffered still more from agony of mind, from
> the separation of God, after Whom they now so bitterly longed.
> They would gladly endure ten thousand years of torment for the
> sake of one second of earthly life in which they might repent and
> be reconciled to Him.[19]

84

All this was in store for those who rejected the lessons of the convent school. Yet, Agnes Repplier remembered how her fears were assuaged by the gentle words and touch of one of her teachers after a particularly descriptive sermon on hell. "'Not for you, Agnes,' she said, 'not for you. Don't be fearful, child!' thus undoing in one glad instant the results of an hour's hard preaching, and sending me comforted to bed."[20]

Sodalities

The sisters also considered sodalities or religious organizations to be crucial agents in the spiritual development of the girls. These groups met at least once a week to receive instruction on spiritual matters from a sister-moderator and to offer special prayers and devotions to their patron and protector, the Blessed Virgin Mary. All the academies encouraged the girls to join these groups.

From its earliest years, the Society of the Sacred Heart emphasized the importance of sodalities in its schools: the Angels, for the youngest children; the St. Aloysians, for those of junior high age; and the Children of Mary, for the older girls. The highest group, the Children of Mary, sought to develop the spiritual life through mental prayer and meditation. Admittance required virtue, exemplary behavior in school, good example and loyalty to the traditions of the Sacred Heart. The elaborate rituals, which marked the reception of a girl into the Children of Mary, included a procession to the chapel; prayers and hymns. The ceremony reached its culmination when the priest placed a religious medal around the neck of the new member. Tradition held that the medal, bearing the image of the Sacred Heart on one side and the Immaculate Conception on the other, revealed a girl's vocation. If the Immaculate Conception faced out when the girl received the medal she would become a mother. The Sacred Heart side meant the convent.

The Children of Mary met once a week for instruction and some form of devotion to Mary. Sodalists from the Academy of the Sacred Heart in Clifton kept weekly notes on the Children of Mary meetings between 1870 and 1910. Throughout the conferences the Mistresses in charge stressed the virtues of humility, obedience, silence, good example to the rest of the school, purity, and manners. In almost every meeting Mary was held up as their model. The girls were encouraged to say the rosary, examine their consciences and visit the Blessed Sacrament daily.[21]

The notes for these sodality meetings reveal how the sisters combined particular virtues with piety. A girl was judged pious and on the path to heaven if she followed convent school etiquette and held convent school values. For the sisters, disregard of academy norms meant rebellion against God and the church. At one sodality meeting, a nun told the girls that by obeying their teachers at school, they followed God's will, because it was through those in authority that one came to know his intentions. In 1881 the Children of Mary learned of the Blessed Mother's hidden life in the temple, where she was obliged to study Hebrew because she spoke only Syro-Chaldean. From her example, the nun reminded the girls of their obligation to speak French faithfully at the required times during the day.

> Although our immediate aim is a worldly one as we wish to become ornamental as well as useful members of society, still we can give great pleasure to the Heart of Jesus by our fidelity to this practice as it forms one of the rules of our school.[22]

In December 1904 the sodalists agreed to speak of the Blessed Virgin at recreation; praise someone they disliked; make three acts of mortification at table; imitate Mary by modesty; practice charity of word and repeat fifty times daily, "O Mary, conceived without sin, pray for us who have recourse to thee."[23]

The Religious of the Sacred Heart also reinforced the bond between piety and conduct for the youngest children, the Angels. Like the Children of Mary, the Angels kept a detailed record of their meetings. The moderator stressed the practices of cheerfulness, promptness, humility, self-control, and obedience and read them passages from the Curé of Ars, the Little Flower, and St. Francis de Sales. In order to remain faithful to their duties and to the Sacred Heart, little girls pinned over their hearts a slip of paper with the inscription

"Jesus of Nazareth, King of my heart." If they failed to fulfill their obligations, they were required to remove it for one hour.[24]

Among the sodalities established in the B.V.M. schools were the Children of Mary, the Sodality of Our Lady of the Sacred Heart, the Holy Angels, and the Rosary Association. The purpose of these groups was threefold: to show devotion to the Blessed Mother, practice purity in her honor, and imitate her as the ideal of womanhood.[25] The Mercy school St. Xavier had a St. Aloysius Sodality of the Immaculate Conception for the older girls and a Holy Angels for the younger students. The Confraternity of the Rosary and the Angelic Warfare formed the two groups for the Dominican academies in Sinsinawa and Madison, Wisconsin.

In addition to sodalities, all Roman Catholic children in these academies were encouraged to enroll in the League of the Sacred Heart. This international organization, founded in Paris in 1844, published *The Messenger of the Sacred Heart* and distributed tiny pamphlets which included intentions for each day of the month. Any Catholic students interested in prayer and spreading devotion to the Sacred Heart could belong. Members from all over the world joined in a communion of reparation on first Friday.

Non-Catholics in the Academies

The religious atmosphere of the convent school would appear to preclude the acceptance of non-Catholic students. Yet Protestants and even Jewish girls attended the academies. Although the schools required their presence at every religious service and class, the nuns reassured the parents that the religious principles of their children would always be respected and no undue influence exercised upon them. Nonetheless, the religious goals of the sisters in educating youth would hardly allow them to neglect the souls of those placed in their care. Though not directly proselytizing, the sisters engaged in a kind of missionary work in their own schools.

Many non-Catholics attended convent schools in Midwestern cities because they had few educational alternatives.

After 1870, when secular high schools began opening in large numbers, non-Catholic enrollment in academies dropped. For example, during the 1850s, the superior of St. Xavier Academy, noted that almost all the children in the select school were Protestant.[26] Yet by the 1870s few non-Catholics attended St. Xavier. Harriet Rose, a pupil at this academy in the late 1840s, typified many of the reasons a Protestant or a Jewish girl might attend a convent school. She began in a public school on the northside of Chicago, but the rough Irish children from "Shantytown" frightened her. The next two private schools closed, leaving the Mercy academy as the only private school near her home. Harriet's father opposed her attendance there but his resistance broke down after his wife's meeting with the sisters. The child loved the nuns and remained there for four years as a boarder and a day student.[27]

The academies of the Sacred Heart usually enrolled the largest number of non-Catholics. The Society's aristocratic reputation overcame many of the reservations that wealthy non-Catholics might have had about sending their daughters to Catholic schools. These parents believed that the academies would teach their girls culture, refinement, manners, and a strong sense of morality as well as keep them safe.[28] Yet even these academies experienced a decline in the attendance of Protestant and Jewish students after 1870. In St. Louis 531 girls enrolled at the Academy of the Sacred Heart between 1841 and 1851; 225 were Protestant. During the 1860s an average of eighteen out of the sixty-four girls registered each year were Protestant.[29] Of the 192 girls enrolled in Clifton during the 1870s, ninety-one were Protestant. The attendance in the next decade rose to 197 with eighty-seven Protestants and four Jewish girls. In the last ten years of the nineteenth century, thirty-two Protestants and one Jewish pupil attended out of a total of 146.[30] The following table gives the religious breakdown of the Academy of the Sacred Heart in Chicago and later Lake Forest, from 1858 to 1920.

Whether few or many non-Catholics were enrolled in the academies, the sisters promised to refrain from suggesting conversion to them. However, no mention of conversion

88

TABLE 6

Academy of the Sacred Heart, Chicago and Lake Forest
1858–1920

	Total	Protestants	Jews
1858–1870	373	131	
1871–1880	360	62	3
1881–1890	414	85	
1891–1900	234	79	
1901–1910	538	109	
1911–1920	294	44	

SOURCE: The Student Register of the Academy of the Sacred Heart at Taylor Street, Chicago and Lake Forest, Archives of the Academy of the Sacred Heart, Lake Forest.

NOTE: This student register also provided a partial list of the various denominations to which the Protestants belonged. In the 1880s, twenty-six Episcopalians, ten Presbyterians, six Methodists, five Unitarians, four Congregationalists, one Universalist and one Baptist enrolled in the academy. From 1901 to 1910, forty-three Episcopalians, eight Congregationalists, six Lutherans, five Baptists, two Presbyterians, and two Methodists attended the Sacred Heart Academy.

was needed. A former Sacred Heart girl wrote of the pervasive influence of Catholicism on Protestants:

> The tender little customs and practices of every hour, the beliefs of their comrades, the lives of the teachers revered and passionately loved, the whole atmosphere of a Religious House—all combine to form an indirect influence as impossible to guard against as difficult afterward to counteract.[31]

A pupil at St. Clara Academy further illustrated the effects of a convent education on a Protestant. The child, Clara Stevens, was intrigued by the catechism classes and religious services she was forced to attend. Catholic beliefs began appearing very reasonable to the young Presbyterian. During a discussion of purgatory she turned to her friend and whispered. "That's the place I've been looking for." "Indeed," said the friend, "well, you're welcome to my part of it."[32] The example of the sisters deeply impressed her. One day she watched the harsh face of one of her teachers become relaxed, soft, and luminous at prayer. "Really and truly, Sister believes in what she is saying! She knows she is talking to God!"[33] A feeling of exclusion from her peers also worked toward Clara's conversion.[34] The girl remembered how she threw herself on the ground and began weeping because she could not receive Holy Communion with the other children on the feast of Corpus Christi. Clara Stevens asked for baptism after three years at the academy. In 1869 she became Sister Charles Borromeo.

The schools staged elaborate celebrations whenever a girl entered the church. Electra Frazier's baptismal ceremony at Maryville Academy on December 8, 1891 began with a candlelit procession through the school which stopped at each shrine of Our Lady. Unfortunately, Electra's white veil caught fire just as the procession reached the statue of Mary in the chapel. Her veil completely burned but she and the other girls escaped injury except for slightly scorched white dresses. A Religious of the Sacred Heart recalled that "an admirable order reigned, the children remained kneeling in perfect silence and the procession was continued as if nothing had happened."[35]

Bringing souls into the Church gave great satisfaction to the sisters. While most of the baptisms that occurred in the convent academies were community celebrations, some took place in secrecy. At Maryville Academy, for example, the Sacred Heart Religious chose to baptize a young girl on her deathbed, without her parents' permission. The sisters sympathized with the sorrow of the family yet noted that "we could look upon it only in the light of a great grace for which endless Magnificats should be sung. . . . we have the immense consolation of having sent a soul to Heaven."[36]

Although proselytizing was not the goal of the academies, when few conversions occurred, the sisters worried about the morality of teaching non-Catholics. The experience of Sister Charles Borromeo is a case in point. As the former Presbyterian who had been deeply affected by her convent education at St. Clara, she knew that nuns exerted a powerful influence on Protestant girls. Following her profession as a Sinsinawa Dominican, she was assigned to a select school in the Midwest where forty-five of the fifty students were Protestant.[37] As in all convent academies, crucifixes and Catholic pictures hung on the walls, all students knelt for Catholic prayers, and the Catholic students recited their catechism aloud during school hours.

For Sister Charles, a nun in these circumstances had a

special duty to influence Protestant pupils. Through the teaching of history and literature, the sisters could expose Protestant girls to Catholic ideas, motives, and principles for moral guidance. If the nuns failed to do "God's special work of infusing faith into their souls," at least they were able to keep Protestant girls pure, noble, and womanly.[38]

Religious Reading

Efforts to form the girls' piety through religious observances, retreats, sodalities, and conversions extended to their reading. The sisters closely monitored every word the children read and provided them with works of a pious nature. The girls read biographies of such figures as Ignatius Loyola, Jeanne de Chantal, Sophie Barat, Francis of Assisi, Elizabeth Seton, Joan of Arc, St. Aloysius, and Francis Xavier. They meditated on the devotional writings of Father F. W. Faber, Francis de Sales, the Little Flower, and John Henry Newman. The popular religious poets in the convent schools included Father Faber, Father Abraham Ryan, Louis Imogen Guiney, and Francis Thompson.[39]

Feminine religious models appeared in classroom readers and library periodicals. Greatest among these heroines was, of course, the Blessed Virgin who embodied all possible womanly perfection. Her purity, humility, submission, self-sacrifice, and charity as both virgin and mother made her the ideal to which all schoolgirls should aspire. Other models included the foundresses of religious orders and saints, such as Catherine of Siena, the Little Flower, Teresa of Avila, and Margaret Mary Alacoque. The most popular women in the literature with the exception of the Virgin Mary were the virgin martyrs of the Early Church.

Beautiful, rich, and aristocratic, the virgin martyr at an early age vowed herself to Jesus Christ. Unfortunately, she attracted pagan senators, governors, and emperors whom she rejected because of her betrothal to Jesus. Invariably, the young woman underwent numerous tortures for her faith and was finally beheaded. This scenario was repeated throughout the literature.

St. Agnes's life represented the ideal of Roman Catholic girlhood. Born to a rich, aristocratic, illustrious Roman family, she experienced a "mystic and ecstatic union with the Heavenly Bridegroom" by the time she was thirteen. The beautiful maiden's rejection of a rich pagan resulted in her appearance before the governor, who was also the spurned man's father. When she refused to renounce her vow of virginity, Agnes was stripped of her clothes and dragged through the street to a brothel. There an angel threw a brilliant light around her and covered her with a snow-white robe. Her suitor died when he touched her. The governor ordered her burned in a fire, but she remained unharmed. Before the executioner's sword ended the young maiden's life, she murmured:

> Jesus! my Spouse! my All! my own Love!
> Am I not Thine alone? Upon my brow
> Hast Thou not left Thy signet? on this hand
> Hast Thou not placed Thy ring—the golden ring,
> Of our divine espousals heavenly pledge?
> Come, O my Love! I long to view Thy face,
> Come, take Thine Agnes to Thine own embrace;
> For ever with the Lord![40]

Accounts of the tortures experienced by the virgin martyrs figured prominently in these stores. Julianna, a wealthy, beautiful daughter of a Roman senator, refused to marry a pagan because of her faith. Though scourged, hanged by the hair, fastened to a wheel with sharp blades, which cut her flesh and bones, scorched in a fire and immersed in burning oil and molten lead, she refused to break her virginal promise to Jesus. Beheading finally ended the tortures.[41] Martinia was whipped, torn with chains, her limbs cut off, rubbed with hot wax and exposed to beasts. Milk and blood flowed from her wounds but she too refused to succumb.[42] The Roman Emperor Diocletian, wanted Philomena for his wife, but his promises and later tortures could not persuade her to renounce her faith.[43]

The story of Cecilia provided another twist in the tales of the virgin martyrs. As a secret convert to Christianity, Cecilia prayed all day and night, helped the poor, mortified her flesh and longed for martyrdom. Her father betrothed her to a brilliant, handsome, young, pagan philosopher. On their wedding night, Cecilia managed not only to convert him but also to preserve her virginity. Later, she received her wish for martyrdom. Her death was depicted in a popular painting: Cecilia knelt with outstretched arms, eyes heavenward and long hair reaching her bare shoulders while her muscular, bearded executioner, clothed in a loincloth, stood over her with a sword raised above his head.[44]

As models of convent school life, the nuns selected virgins like themselves. The books and periodicals they allowed in the academy presented virginity as the highest state of life for Catholic women. Though the nuns paid lip service to the cultured, pious homemaker, she rarely assumed heroic proportions. Married women only appeared as models for Catholic girls if they had suffered because of marriage. A story published in *The Messenger of the Sacred Heart* in 1884 portrayed a young woman of the Early Church who felt no call to virginity. Although she realized her heart was inclined to a less high rather than a noble state, she was determined to pay for her cowardice.[45] She married a man whom she detested and led a miserable life with him. In another story set in France, a dying father forced his daughter to wed, despite her desire to enter a convent. Her worthless husband dueled, gambled, spent all her money, beat and humiliated her. His death and that of her beloved child allowed the woman finally to embrace religious life.[46] Yet another story published in 1910 portrayed a convent school girl in America who rejected a vocation and married a lukewarm Catholic. He stopped attending Mass, lost his wealth and disappeared, leaving her to raise their daughter alone. The husband returned many years later with a large fortune he had made in Australia. However, the woman died a few weeks later, the daughter entered the convent, and the reformed husband became a Dominican brother.[47]

Religious Writings

The girls responded heartily to the books they read and the models presented to them. Religious themes dominated their poetry, essays, book reviews, and historical articles. The piety in their writings reflected a combination of forces present in the convent school.

The Blessed Virgin captured the imagination of the girls. Countless articles were written about her appearances, her virtues, the dogma of the Immaculate Conception, her shrines and churches, the miracles attributed to her, and Marian devotions. A typical article described the admiration of Catholic poets for the Virgin.[48] Another encouraged devotion to Mary through the angelus, the *memorare*, seven sorrows, sodalities, the wearing of the scapular, litanies, celebration of her feasts, and most of all, through the rosary. "Yes, indeed, our beads are the links of a golden chain which binds us closely to Our Blessed Savior and His dear Mother."[49] Mary was also an intercessor for these girls. One should pray to her more than any other saint because God can never refuse anything she asks.

> If upon the sea of life we are threatened with shipwreck on some rock of temptation, we should remember the Star of the Sea and look to her for guidance. If night seems to cast its shadows around us, let us turn to the beautiful Morning Star, and darkness will speedily disperse.[50]

Most of all, the Blessed Virgin functioned as the model of perfect womanhood for convent girls in her role of pure virgin and suffering mother.

Other saints also appealed to convent school pupils. Numerous poems celebrated St. Agnes and St. Cecilia. An academy girl in 1895 wrote of Agnes: "O Holy Virgin, spotless maid/White Flow's of stainless purity."[51] Aloysius Gonzaga was another favorite of the girls even though the pupils rarely looked to male saints as their models of sanctity or inspiration. In the eyes of the girls he appeared to have transcended his sex because of his vow of virginity at the age of nine and his entrance into the Jesuits at sixteen. A model of purity and innocence, Aloysius Gonzaga died when he was twenty-three. An 1878 poem by Eleanor Donnely on the feast of "The Angelic Saint," patron of her sodality, described the young Gonzaga.

But he bore himself so purely
Like a lily white and fresh,
They called him—"The little prince exempt
From the weaknesses of the flesh."
And though his soul's bright venture
Was such as seraphs wear,
He yielded up his young life
To penance and to prayer.

Oh! say not, precious children
"Such heights are not for us!"
He loved Our Lord intensely,
And Our Lord is generous.
'Ere the light of grace auspicious
In your tender souls grows dim,
Come to St. Aloysius,
And learn to love like him.[52]

Convent school girls enjoyed the idea of saints suffering for their love of God. Ruth Fox voiced the longing of the girls for this pain.

Thou wouldst have us know
That the soul's perfume is by pain set free;
Thou makest suffering our daily part,
For out of sorrow richest blessings flow.[53]

Mabelle Clarke Bredette, a sophomore at St. Clara's, hoped to imitate Jesus in Gethsemane.

O, Jesus this my prayer, my heart's request,
For I am blind and know not what is best
When in my own Gethsemane, be mine
The holy grace to add, "Not my will, Lord, but Thine."[54]

But the greatest pain for the schoolgirl was separation from God. The poem "Domine Non Sum Dignus" appeared in an 1893 newspaper published by the St. Xavier girls.

But, now, dear Lord, the cruel pain,
Which seems my very soul to tear,
While far from Thee I thus remain,
Grows all too great for me to bear.

My God, my life, it must not be,
'Twere death to live, from Thee apart;
I'll bring my sins my misery,
And bury all within Thy Heart.[55]

While romanticizing spiritual suffering, the girls also expressed resistance to a pursuing God. A great favorite among them was Francis Thompson's "Hound of Heaven." In this poem a reluctant soul tried for years to hide from God but finally, after countless struggles, was captured by divine love. The poem appealed to the girls because it combined an adolescent need for freedom with the realization that submission ultimately would be their lot. A convent school girl saw in Thompson's poem the Catholic view of life and its true solution. "Created things cannot satisfy the human heart. Perfect liberty and complete happiness are found only in God."[56]

Convent girls savored the idea of being pursued by a relentless suitor. Succumbing to divine love and suffering for its sake sparked many romantic fantasies. The virgin mother and the virgin martyr symbolized these ideals though neither virgin motherhood nor physical martyrdom were possible. The girls transformed these symbols into the attainable goals of virginal purity, spiritual motherhood, martyrdom of earthly desire and marriage to the "heavenly spouse."

In convent school poetry, Jesus Christ became the relentless lover, the bridegroom and the spouse. His call could not be resisted.

> I was a child amid my father's field;
>   A voice as coming from the tree-tops tall
> Or wild winds blown from far-off, lonely wealds,
>   Was whispering to me, "Leave all! Leave all!" . . .
>
> And all was left to follow where it led,
>   That sweet, dread voice that held my soul in thrall;
> Since then, dear Master, in thy footsteps red
>   I walk with heavenly joy, my God, my All![57]

Desires for self-sacrifice, love, commitment, and romance coalesced in the attitude toward religious vocation. "My Spouse," a poem in a 1906 issue of *The Young Eagle* from St. Clara Academy expressed these desires:

> 'Twas by a lov'd and only son
> My wayward heart was wooed and won.
> Just how he did, I cannot say;
> 'Twas such a sweet, persuasive way. . . .

"My child," said He, "give Me thy heart;
Be thine to choose the better part.
Come, follow Me, and leave all strife;
I am the Way, the Truth, the Life." . . .

I'll follow Thee, what'er my lot,
My life were drear where Thou are not!
I thus become the happy bride
Of God the Son, the Crucified.[58]

Convent schoolgirls celebrated the reception and profession of postulants and novices in their newspapers. In one enthusiastic account, the writer carefully described the candidates dressed in white, their entrance to the hymn "Veni Creator," and their acceptance of a scapular, cincture, rosary, mantle, white lace veil, and crown of flowers. The academy observer was most impressed by the chanting of "Ante Christi" while the newly professed prostrated themselves before the altar.[59] Another story, covering the reception of postulants, discussed three young souls who elected to leave the world and its unhallowed spirit in order to devote themselves more completely to the service of God. The girls of St. Clara dedicated a poem to the "chosen twelve" on their reception day, the feast of St. Dominic.

Twelve virgins fair to-day He chose
So sweet, so fair, in bride's array,
Pure hearts, that now in His repose
Espoused to Him, on this saint's day. . . .

From this dear Heart you'll never part.
Each year will add its crown of love.
'Tis heaven, dear Heart, where'er Thou art.
'Tis heav'n on earth, 'tis heaven above.[60]

Similar sentiments appeared in the national Catholic press. In 1892, *The Messenger of the Sacred Heart* published "A Novice's Reception into the Society of the Sacred Heart."

Before a lowly Altar Throne
    Bedecked in garlands fair,
        The music floats
        In swelling notes
    And incense fills the air,
    Oh, beautiful the bright array!
    On earth it is a bridal day. . . .

> "My God, yes, I'm forever Thine,"
> The bride cries, "Thine alone!
>   Oh, enter Thou
>   This temple now
> which Thou hast made Thine own,
> Thou the Annointing Spirit art:
> To Thee I leave each aching heart."[61]

Marriage, motherhood, or worldly achievement never could surpass the supreme honor of choosing religious life. The beautiful, rich, young woman who left all for the love of God was the unchallenged idol of the academy. Antonia White's convent schoolgirl knew well that a

> vocation was to be more ardently desired and more warmly accepted than anything in the world. A secular life, however pious, however happy, was only the wretched crust with which Catholics who were not called to the grace of religious life must nourish themselves as best they could. A vocation followed was the supreme good, a vocation rejected, the supreme horror.[62]

Conclusion

Religious devotions, practices, and ideals dominated the convent school world. Like every other aspect of academy life under their control, the nuns used piety to form the girls according to conventual notions of true Catholic womanhood. This entailed the cultivation of the so-called feminine virtues of self-sacrifice, humility, submission, purity, silence, and obedience as well as the equation of piety with adherence to convent school values.[63] The efforts of the nuns were aided by the daily examination of conscience, frequent confession, and retreats. These practices encouraged conformity to the wishes of the nuns and reminded the girls of the very serious consequences of failure.

Convent school piety reinforced the Church's position that the religious stood higher in the scale of perfection than the married. Marriage seemed to afford fewer opportunities than the convent for heroism. Convent school girls romanticized the suffering and sacrifice, which they believed characterized the life of a nun, and pious literature reminded them that no one rivaled the sanctity of the woman who spurned marriage and motherhood for the convent.

Most importantly, this religious system was designed to keep the girls faithful to conventual values long after graduation. In addition to fostering a deep piety in their students, the nuns sought to regulate their behavior by equating the repudiation of academy values and standards with loss of the Catholic faith. No higher stakes could have been set. Convent school graduates who fulfilled the expectations of their teachers were assured of eternal life. Those who rejected them endangered their souls. A choice of career or lifestyle entailed far more than earthly considerations.

Expectations and Reality   5

Introduction

$\mathcal{T}$hrough academic, social, and spiritual training, convent school girls learned from their teachers what was expected of them after leaving school. The Catholic periodicals allowed in the academies and the clerical visitors to the school reinforced and expanded upon the sisters' teaching. Students responded to this advice in their school newspapers and magazines, while graduates expressed their reactions in their careers and writings. Whether former convent school girls embraced or rejected the approved roles, they were deeply affected by the expectations of the nuns, the Catholic press, and the clergy.

Expectations

The Sisters

The sisters encouraged religious vocations in their schools and hoped that some of their pupils would enter the convent. These women had no quarrel with the Church's position that celibacy surpassed marriage in the hierarchy of vocations. When the B.V.M.'s in 1893 published a book of literary selections entitled *Woman: A Collection of Tributes to*

Woman, they included a passage from John Lancaster Spalding, bishop of Peoria, which described the nun as the most perfect imitation of Christ. According to Spalding, Christ did not

> exalt intellect and enterprise, and heroic daring, but gentleness, and lovingness, and sweet chastity. He clothed the weak in Heavenly panoply, when he placed purity above strength, and humility above pride. And woman, without father or mother, or brother or sister, loving Christ only, and the children whom he loved, and the poor and the sick, is the heavenliest image of God's charity and tender mercy that walks the earth.[1]

Many nuns also directly recruited Catholic students to take the veil. Sister Mary Genevieve Granger, a Sister of Mercy in Chicago, reminded a former pupil about her intention to enter the convent in 1856.

> Do you ever think of the last conversation we had the day you left St. Agatha's? But I suppose you forgot all about that amidst the many endearments of a sweet home, with cherished Parents, a loved Sister and a kind Brother, but never lose sight, dearest Kate, of that still *Sweeter Home* in Heaven whither we all aspire, and where "Virgin follows the Lamb whithersoever he goeth singing a Canticle which none but themselves can sing."[2]

Later, as religious orders opened more schools, the sisters made even stronger efforts to secure vocations. The mother generals of both the B.V.M.'s and the Sinsinawa Dominicans instructed all their sisters to recruit young women. In 1917 Mother Samuel Coughlin of the Sinsinawa Dominicans required each convent to appoint a sister to the job of vocation director. These sisters were instructed to take aside likely candidates and to discuss with them the possibility of religious life.[3] Mother Isabella, the B.V.M. superior, feared that her sisters were not aggressively encouraging girls to enter the community. She reminded them in 1922 that every sister should obtain one or more vocations to carry on her work.[4]

If a woman could not attempt the most perfect imitation of Jesus Christ, the sisters expected her to be a wife and mother. Yet the nuns knew little more than the girls about marriage, sex, men, and child-bearing and never discussed these subjects with their students. The B.V.M.'s presented a nun's view of the homemaker in their previously mentioned book, *Woman: A Collection of Tributes to Woman.* They dedicated this work to their Davenport, Iowa alumnae. In the introduction a sister reminded her students, past and present, that their mission was to "rescue the fallen scepter of Eve, and restore the old-time harmony by softening the rigor of justice, and melting sternness into love."[5] Immaculate Conception girls could achieve this goal by helping, refining, counseling and loving their husbands and children in the home. "The heart of true womanhood knows where its own sphere is, and never seeks to stray beyond it."[6] A favorite image used by the writers chosen by the B.V.M.'s was the flower which never courted the sun or the light but decayed and died if exposed.

> So woman, born to dignify retreat,
> Unknown to flourish, and unseen be great;
> To give domestic life its sweetest charm,
> With softness, polish, and with virtue warm,
> Fearful of fame, unwilling to be known,
> Should seek but Heaven's applause and her own.[7]

Above all, the sisters expected the wife and mother to sacrifice and suffer for her family. A woman's glory and the end for which she was sent into this world was to live for others and often to die for them.

> Her lot is on you—silent tears to weep
>   And patient smiles to wear through
>   sufferings' hour,
> And sunless riches from affections deep
>   To pour on broken reeds—a wasted
>   shower!
> And to make idols, and to find them clay,
> And to bewail that worship: therefore pray!
>
> Her lot is on you—to be found untried
>   Watching the stars out by the bed of pain,
> With a pale cheek, and yet a brow inspired,
>   And a true heart of hope, though hope be
>   vain;
> Meekly to bear with wrong, to cheer decay,
> And, oh, to love through all things: therefore
>   pray![8]

A Dominican sister from St. Clara Academy in Sinsinawa added to the B.V.M. portrait of the homemaker. Sister Charles Borromeo Stevens, like the writers in the B.V.M. book, insisted that the home was woman's natural sphere yet admitted that domestic life was commonplace and filled with drudgery. Her advice to the woman with an educated mind and religiously trained heart was to keep domestic and household realities in their proper realm and remember that although the house was the center of her material life, the realm of "infinite space" also existed:

> To be "bounded by a nutshell" is, in fact, woman's destiny, her normal condition, and she must submit, as gracefully and wisely, as her peculiarities of disposition and varied traits of character will permit. Physically, materially, she is circumscribed by very narrow boundaries, but intellectually she is not thus restricted; and if she may not go as deep into some things as man, she can go as far, and better still, as high.[9]

Stevens gave no hints as to how the housewife could achieve this goal but reminded her of the rewards of patient and loving submission to household restrictions.

> Some happy day we shall, in our upward flight, draw near the great Golden Gates, which some beloved one of earth, or some blessed one of Heaven, shall have left ajar for us, and, entering in, we shall rest—forevermore—from the toils of the nutshell, and enjoy for all eternity the freedom of infinite space.[10]

Another Sinsinawa Dominican educator, Sister Mary Ruth, also insisted that a woman's rightful place was in the home. At a 1917 meeting of the Catholic Educational Association, this nun criticized women's colleges which trained students for careers outside the home and taught subjects unrelated to homemaking, such as higher mathematics and Greek. In Sister Mary Ruth's opinion, Catholic women's colleges must prepare their pupils for the role of the cultured Catholic homemaker. They must not imitate secular women's schools which emphasized the possibilities of community service, opportunities for club membership, and obligations of a wide social nature.

> Woman must be educated, not to find her delight as a solitary with her books as her best companions, but in the center of the

home where she must make herself and her home so attractive as to charm the home folk; so that her husband will hasten from his place of business and her sons and daughters will hasten from school, all to join the home circle.[11]

A religious vocation, however, absolved a Catholic woman from the duties of the home. Sister Charles Borromeo Stevens believed that only in the convent could an educated and pious Catholic girl find real happiness and fulfilment. She wrote that the majority of educated Catholic women were denied suitable companionship and congenial surroundings because few Catholic men received comparable schoolings.[12]

> Blessed above all others is the educated woman who has a religious vocation. Within convent walls, she finds all that a cultured heart and mind can desire—the surroundings, the companionship, the work that suits her needs and gratifies her tastes. While her heart is fed with peace and joy from the altar table, her mind is fed with inspirations from the throne of God, and she finds earth the vestibule of heaven.[13]

Despite the curriculum changes in the late 19th century which gave convent-trained women other options, it appears that most convent school teachers still expected their students to become either nuns or homemakers. However, some of these teachers might have held different attitudes toward the role of a Catholic woman in society and encouraged their students to think about alternate careers. As will be seen later in the chapter, convent schoolgirls did not dream only of becoming nuns and homemakers, nor did all of them embrace this lifestyle. Unfortunately, no hard evidence exists that indicates a dissenting view among the sisters in regard to women's roles.

The Catholic Press and Clergy

Along with the sisters, the Catholic periodicals read by the students shaped the schoolgirls' thoughts about future roles. Catholic writers agreed with academy teachers that a girl could aspire to no higher state of life than that of the nun. However, these writers concentrated more on delineating the duties and functions of the woman in the home and warning against the dangers of female suffrage than in encouraging religious vocations.[14]

Throughout the period under study, those who wrote for Catholic periodicals generally held common assumptions about women. They believed that Christianity was the first movement in history to give dignity to women and that the church, more than any other institution, protected and defended the weaker sex. Except for the convent, a female's only rightful place was in the home, where she reared children and cared for her husband.[15] A true woman devoted herself only to homemaking.

> Woman's ordinary task, however, will always be the making of home. The long years of maternity, the best part of her life, will leave little time for outward occupations. Her work is to socialize the home, to make of it the genial and diffusive center of happiness and holiness and blessings which extend in ever-widening ripples through all her neighborhood . . .[16]

Catholic writers clearly defined a woman's duties in each stage of her life. A girl showed reverence and submission to her parents and humbly devoted herself to the duties of the home. A married woman knew that her husband was the head of the family, just as Christ was the head of the church. In addition to concentrating on her spouse's temporal and spiritual interests, she also accepted the sacred gift of maternity. Through the penalties of childbirth, she expiated her portion of the sin of Eve.[17]

The belief that woman's place was in the home and her role adjunct to man's was deeply rooted in Catholic culture. Few Catholics dissented from this view. Unsurprisingly, the Catholic press in America was deeply disturbed by the prospect of female suffrage. They used many of the same arguments as non-Catholic opponents of women's suffrage. Catholic writers, like non-Catholic anti-suffragists, predicted the destruction of the family and the home if women were to gain the vote. For example, in 1869 the *Catholic World* wrote that if women were allowed to vote, many would neglect and disdain the simple domestic virtues and duties of wives and mothers. They would become active in politics and run for office. Those who departed from the destiny of wife and mother would disrupt family life and ruin the social fabric of society. "All history proves that the corruptist epochs in a nation's life are precisely those in which women have mingled most in political affairs, and have had the most influence in their management."[18] In 1867, *Ave Maria* foresaw a complete break between the sexes, leading to the defilement and degradation of the weaker sex. Women would lose everything that the Church had gained for them.[19] Even as late as 1915 *America* published an article which predicted the destruction of American society if suffrage passed. Women's exposure to the dangers of the vote would rob them of their perfect womanhood and destroy true motherhood. The writer feared the ultimate consequence of this political equality.

> Women should awaken to the hideous peril they are beckoning into their lives. In proportion as they lose their appeal on men's ideals, they will unleash his brute passions. Then equality will violently pass into inferiority. Let the grim significance of the outrageous assaults, so frequently and recently perpetuated by men on the persons of female seekers of suffrage, be duly appreciated. If women stir up the volcano of man's lower nature, they must expect to suffer by the ensuing eruption. It is only by being superior to man, that they can be safe from him, worshipped by him, and helpful to him; not by being equal. Modern equality is a huge step toward ancient inferiority.[20]

Even a former Sacred Heart convent school girl, Katherine Conway, spoke against suffrage. A well-known journalist and Irish-American community figure, Conway wrote, "It seems so beyond question that woman, as woman, can have no vocation to public life . . . it cannot be necessary, or even useful, that she should try to do what she cannot do."[21]

Catholic writers diverged from non-Catholic anti-suffragists when they blamed Protestant reformers for women's rights agitation. According to this view, Protestants, since the Reformation, had repressed women by diminishing the sanctity of marriage and rejecting the values of conventual life. In 1872, the *Catholic World* charged that the campaign for female suffrage was the result of three centuries of Protestant oppression:

> The broad river of women's influence, flowing so calmly and majestically through the centuries of the church's undisturbed

unity, has been damned up by the Protestant tradition of the last 300 years, until it has broken forth again as a turbulent torrent, devastating where it once fertilized, disturbing where once it conciliated. In its new form and strange aggressiveness, it now horrifies mankind, where in earlier days, in its legitimate sphere, it guided the greatest statesmen, orators and saints, and gravely helped them on the road to heaven, to science and to happiness.[22]

Martha More Avery, a former radical and famous Catholic convert, also viewed female suffrage in religious terms. Not only was the crusade for the women's vote a legacy of the Protestant Reformation, but it was a plot hatched by the devil himself, in opposition to Christianity.[23]

The arguments in the press against woman suffrage reflected the views of most American Catholic bishops and clergymen. In 1900 the National American Woman Suffrage Association could only name six Catholic clergymen in America who supported this cause. These were the priests J. W. Dalton, Thomas Scully and Edward McGlynn and the bishops John Ireland of St. Paul, Bernard McQuaid of Rochester, and John Lancaster Spalding of Peoria.[24] The large majority of American Catholic priests and bishops agreed with the position of the ardent anti-feminist, James Cardinal Gibbons (1834–1921). Gibbons, the leading American ecclesiastic of the later nineteenth and early twentieth centuries, spoke against women's rights throughout his career. In 1886 he wrote that the only threat to women was the demand for equal rights.[25] Speaking before an audience at his Baltimore cathedral in 1900, the cardinal denounced woman suffrage.

I regard "woman's rights" as the worst enemies of the female sex. They rob woman of all that is amiable and gentle, tender and attractive, they rob her of her innate grace of character, and give her nothing in return but masculine boldness and brazen effrontery. They are habitually preaching about woman's rights and perogatives, and have not a word to say about her duties and responsibilities. They withdraw her from those obligations which properly belong to her sex and fill her with ambition to usurp positions for which neither God nor nature ever intended her.[26]

As late as 1920 Gibbons opposed women's entrance into the political arena. Other prominent critics of women's rights, such as Archbishop John Glennon of St. Louis, added to the debate. In 1912 Glennon wrote that he feared if women were granted the right to vote, they would revolutionize society and liberate themselves from all laws. In their quest to become full citizens and leaders, women would sunder the bonds of marriage and motherhood. The archbishop believed that nuns had a special mission in regard to these "modern" women.

> It is to combat these, that we need Catholic American Sisters to teach their Catholic sisters that Catholic virtues still may grow—still must bloom, here in America; that graciousness, gentleness, faith and devotion are and will remain a woman's chiefest ornaments—that in them lies her best and fittest education.[27]

Clerical Visitors

Through Catholic periodicals, academy girls were well aware that bishops and other prominent Catholics regarded female suffrage as unnatural. Academy commencements provided yet another forum for anti-feminist views. Commencement speakers delivered a final warning to young women about their proper role outside the academy walls. Mt. St. Joseph graduates in Dubuque and St. Clara girls in Sinsinawa listened to the pleas of clergy and laymen to recognize their true place in society and reject the claims of the suffragettes. These men reminded the girls that their only true sphere was the home if not called to the higher life of a nun.

A theme common to all these speakers was God's creation of women for different purposes than those for which he created men. Therefore, women possessed different rights and duties than men. Archbishop Sebastian Messmer of Milwaukee sounded this note in his 1911 address to St. Clara graduates:

> I say it is just as much God's law and the fundamental demand of nature itself, that women hold another position than man and man a different position from that of woman. Her vocation is not the same in everything as that of man. The purpose for which God made her is a different one from that for which man has been created, and consequently her duties are different, her rights are different, and her position is different.[28]

The archbishop of Milwaukee believed that since the bible and the church enjoined women to obey men and take an inferior position to them, no power on earth could give women equal rights to men in social, political, and public realms. Speaking at this same school eight years later, Archbishop John T. McNicholas of Cincinnati reminded the girls of the different nature and function of the sexes when he asserted that right reason, revealed truth, and the teachings of the Roman Catholic Church all placed women in the home.[29] Archbishop P. J. Garrigan of Sioux City, Iowa, exhorted Mt. St. Joseph graduates never to forget that the economy of creation and the providence of God best fitted them for their "natural sphere" of the home and domestic life.[30] The ideal woman, according to William Onahan, a prominent Chicago Catholic layman who addressed St. Clara Academy in 1913, "loves her home, is devoted to her family and scrupulously faithful to the grave responsibilities of her position."[31] Another speaker at Sinsinawa in 1911 defined the true woman as the mother of the race, the sister of men, the wife of men, and the consecrated virgin among men. "Those thoughts, those facts, are the most significant in the life of a woman, and wherever woman fails to be what she should be, it is because she fails to be a true, a strong, a valiant mother, sister, wife, or religious."[32]

The woman who failed to embrace the roles of nun or mother and wife was scorned by the commencement speakers. Archbishop Garrigan described the "new woman," the "manly woman," the "smart girl," as an abnormal growth, not a genuine feminine development. The archbishop of Dubuque, John J. Keane, a strong opponent of woman suffrage, deplored the tendencies he discerned among the advocates of woman's rights and pleaded with Mt. St. Joseph girls in 1912 to reject all of their claims.

> Oh, for more stability in woman's life, more persistent clinging to the good and safe, a keener sensitiveness of the duties of true womanhood, and a disgust for the follies and fads that promise crudeness and mannishness. I would be surprised and disappointed if any of the young women I see before me today should

become such. I am surprised at some of the things I see and hear. I am not a pessimist but I like not all the things I see in this age and I see a tendency to revert to savagery.[33]

The commencement speakers naturally feared the consequences of women getting the vote and praised Cardinal Gibbons's position on women. Messmer believed that a woman had the greatest influence on public affairs when she confined herself to her God-given position in society and stayed out of political affairs, which were beyond her sphere.[34] Onahan's true woman exercised her power by way of the home. "Woman may be destined to save the country, not indeed by the ballot, but by the right and rule of the home and family; her legitimate influence is there, not in the glare and the limelight of public notice.[35]

In the classroom, in the pages of the Catholic press and speeches and statements of the clergy, convent school girls were reminded of their duty to become nuns or homemakers. While their teachers focused upon religious vocation and the cultured homemaker, the press and the clergy outlined the duties and qualities of the woman in the home and warned against the extraordinary danger of women forgetting these obligations. Together, these forces waged a valiant battle to keep Catholic women harnassed to the two traditional female careers sanctioned by the church.

Educated non-Catholic women, on the other hand, were exposed to the ideals of "true womanhood" as well as more expansive notions of women's roles in society. Smith College's president L. Clark Seeyle expressed the common ideal of the educated woman in the 1890s: "The college is not intended to fit woman for any particular sphere or profession but to develop by the most carefully devised means all her intellectual capacities, so that she may be a more perfect woman in any position."[36] Although secular educators still held onto the feminine model of serving society as educated wives and mothers until the early twentieth century, they also encouraged women to move beyond the familial sphere and experiment in other fields.[37]

Reaction of the Girls

Convent schoolgirls knew what was expected of them after leaving the academy, yet they held varied opinions about women's roles and their future careers. In their newspapers, speeches, and debates, the girls often discussed these issues. During the nineteenth century the students held positions quite similar to their teachers, the Catholic press, and the Catholic hierarchy. However, by the twentieth century, the girls began to take issue with the traditional church line.[38]

In the 1880s Mt. St. Joseph girls and St. Clara girls sharply criticized those women who failed to embrace the approved roles. A Mt. St. Joseph student in 1883 asked where a woman's true sphere lay and answered that it was not in the affairs of state but in the heart of the family, the home circle. She recognized the gift of some women for teaching and lecturing and their desire to use this talent for the benefit of others. Yet the writer noted that women should remember that charity begins at home "and if each mother and sister endeavor to prevent evil in their own household, there will be little need for public lectures."[39] The 1884 valedictorian of St. Clara addressed the question "What a Girl Ought To Do in the World?" She declared that the girls wanted to "do right, to see what is beautiful in the world, to make others happy, to help our needy brethren."[40] Any girl with a career in mind, ambitions or desires for fame was "unnatural" since a girl's first aspiration must be to make the home a pleasant, happy refuge. The valedictorian regarded women's rights as vulgar and prayed to be struck deaf and blind before joining the suffragettes.

While convent schoolgirls never questioned the primacy of the nun or the homemaker in their discussions of women and suffrage, they did acknowledge the value of the single woman. This was no small accomplishment, considering that the nuns, the Catholic press, and the clergy pretended the single woman did not exist. At a St. Xavier alumnae banquet in 1889, an unmarried graduate declared that maidens possessed no single right or privilege that their married sisters did not have to a higher degree, yet they were content and would not exchange their single state for marriage. In her role as a "sweet, amiable, altogether delightful old maid," the speaker predicted that men would "wonder what could have been the matter with them to allow so much worth to slip through their clumsy fingers."[41] In 1892 a Xavier pupil wrote that the ideal woman may be a mother, a nun or an "advocate of single blessedness." According to this girl, the unmarried woman frequently "proves to be a sweet, sympathetic and true friend, too courageous to fear the stigma of leading a single life."[42]

In addition to recognizing the worth of the single woman, Xavier girls held strong opinions on women's rights and suffrage. In April of 1893 these students debated the question of whether a woman could become president of the United States. Those against the proposition based their arguments on woman's natural sphere and man's greater physical strength and passions. The supporters of a female president believed that since women studied at the best universities with men and worked at many of the same jobs, a woman would soon be elected to the highest office in the land. In the next round of debates, the anti-suffragist team discussed the distractions of the home and God's creation of woman as subordinate to man. The respondent acknowledged the role played by women as wives and mothers but noted that the single woman could occupy their time by holding public service jobs. She agreed that God commanded Eve to be subject to Adam yet argued that this injunction applied only to Eve and not all women. She also dismissed St. Paul's instructions to females in the New Testament as rules of behavior for early Christian times, not as God's will. The Xavier girl wrote: "The acknowledgement of woman's equality with man is of too great importance to have its fate rest on the figurative allusions of the Bible."[43]

By the turn of the century, convent schoolgirls no longer adhered to the traditional Catholic position on the role of women. In addition to acknowledging the value of the single woman, academy students advocated greater involvement for women in affairs of state. Still, convent-trained girls were reluctant to challenge the primacy of the nun and the home-maker. In 1905, for example, a St. Clara girl admitted that a woman had duties to the state, but she couched these responsibilities in domestic terms. The true woman, she believed, secured order, comfort, and adornment both in the home and in the state.[44]

In their arguments over women's rights, academy girls reflected the growing acceptance of female suffrage that was occurring in society at large. However, they were careful to strike a balance between women's domestic duties and her concern for society. The Mt. St. Joseph newspaper, *The Labarium*, expressed the typical convent school endorsement of suffrage. In 1912, a student wrote that the criticism against the woman vote was based on the reasonable protest that woman's sphere was the home and that her dignity, purity, power, and influence would be destroyed by the vote. She countered this argument by noting that those who back suffrage do so not because they want to throw off domestic duties but "because they feel that their voices raised for the benefit of society might, if united with that of noble-minded men, overrule those who seem bent on lowering the standard of political and social morality."[45] If women voted, conditions in American society would improve while women would retain their love and devotion to the home and hold the respect due to their exalted positions as mothers and guides of the race.[46]

Prior to World War I, academy publications contained numerous examples that convent schoolgirls no longer clung to traditional church teachings on the role of women. The teachers apparently granted their girls a certain degree of autonomy in expressing opinions which departed from conventional Catholic attitudes toward women's roles. The 1911 class prophecy from St. Xavier Academy revealed that convent schoolgirls dreamed of careers beyond that of nun or mother and wife. Indeed, according to this prediction only two girls from the class chose motherhood and one, convent life. The others envisioned themselves in such careers as poet, actress, teacher, cartoonist, opera singer, hairdresser, suffragette, mayor of a large city, the first Chicago suffragette alderwoman and the president of a woman's club.[47]

In most of the academies under study, girls expressed dissatisfaction with the idea that Catholic women were expected to become either nuns or mothers. The next section examines how the girls conformed to or rejected convent school expectations and whether any graduates pursued their schoolgirl dreams.

Reality

Convent school graduates steered a middle course between traditional expectations and schoolgirl hopes and opinions.[48] The majority became homemakers and nuns, although a sizeable number pursued careers and remained single, an option rarely discussed by the nuns or the clergy. Indeed, available statistics on academy graduates indicate that while at least fifty percent of them married, the percentage of single women was exceedingly high. In some academies, twice as many graduates remained single as chose religious life.

Table 7 illustrates the choices made by graduates of eight convent academies. Unfortunately, only four of the academies could provide information on the precise number of students who married or remained single. The other schools just recorded religious vocations.

The Married Woman

Although most convent school girls chose marriage, for some this decision was probably more difficult than selecting the convent. Separated from their families as well as from members of the opposite sex during their adolescent years, the girls lived more like nuns than young women preparing for marriage. By their elevation of celibacy over wedlock, their glorification of Mary's virginity, and their praise for the virgin martyrs who suffered tortures and death rather than lose their virginity through marriage, the nuns and the clergy encouraged negative attitudes toward matrimony. In choosing marriage, many graduates felt they violated conventual

ideals of purity. Such attitudes, together with a lack of preparation for the physical aspects of marriage, often made the
early years of wedded life painful and trying ones for the
pious woman and her spouse.

TABLE 7

Lifestyles of Academy Graduates

	Students	Married	Single	Religious
Immaculate Conception, 1871–1901	132	51%	32%	17%
Mt. Carmel, Wichita, 1891–1925	229	57%	37%	6%
Mt. St. Joseph, 1874–1920	476			
Sacred Heart, Maryville, 1873–1920	347	65%	26%	10%
Sacred Heart, Villa Duchesne, 1903–1920	165	73%	17%	7%
Sacred Heart, Clifton, 1871–1921	190			15%
St. Clara Academy, 1867–1900	137			19%
St. Xavier Academy, 1873–1900	163			20%

SOURCE: Immaculate Conception Academy published a list of graduates from 1870 to 1911. Mt.
Carmel Alumnae Association compiled a list of graduates from 1891 to 1935, ABVM. The Clark
College Alumnae Association Files in Dubuque contained the names of all students at Mt. St.
Joseph Academy but did not have a complete record of their marital status. Maryville College of
the Sacred Heart published an alumnae directory in 1968, including the names of students from
the classes fo 1873 to 1968. Villa Duchesne/City House (academies of the Sacred Heart in St.
Louis) published an alumnae directory in 1978 beginning with the class of 1903. I found the
names of students who became nuns in Clifton in the Student Register of the Academy of the
Sacred Heart, Clifton, ARSCJ. The number of vocations from St. Clara Academy was obtained
by matching the names of the graduates with those who entered the community, as listed in the
book of entrants and departures, AOP. (Sister Eva McCarty, O.P. provided a figure of 22%
vocations from St. Clara College alumnae between the years 1902 and 1922 in her book *The
Sinsinawa Dominicans*, p. 281). St. Xavier Quarterly, an alumnae publication appearing in January
1921 gave the names of those entering the convent from each class at St. Xavier, ASM. Non-
Catholic students were not included in the percentage of students becoming nuns but were
included in the married/single figures.

NOTE: A higher percentage of academy graduates remained unmarried than the general female
population. In 1910, 71 percent of all women between twenty-five and twenty-nine were married
while 80 percent of females between thirty-five and forty-four were wed. Department of Commerce, Bureau of the Census, *Thirteenth Census of the United States, 1910: Abstract*, p. 149. (See
Table 20 in the Appendix for the marriage rates of the general female population between the
years 1890 and 1920.) The graduates of Maryville and Villa Duchesne were all past the age of
forty-four when their alumnae directories were compiled, whereas the youngest women included in the survey of Immaculate Conception Academy and Mt. Carmel were twenty-eight years
old.
    Female graduates of secular colleges in this period also had a lower marriage rate than the
general female population. However, these women sharply differed from convent school graduates in that they spent many more years in school and were prepared for a variety of professional
careers. Willystine Goodsell, *The Education of Women* (New York: The Macmillan Co., 1923) and
Roberta Frankfort, *Collegiate Woman: Domesticity and Career in Turn of the Century America* (New
York: New York University Press, 1977).

Many married graduates remained strongly attached to
the convent school through the sodalities. These groups met

116

once or twice a month for general religious instructions, services and conferences given by a priest and a nun. Once a month members attended Sunday Mass together and each year they went away for a retreat. They also worked together for charitable causes.[49]

As membership figures for the Children of Mary make clear, a sizeable number of married graduates strongly valued the religious and moral lessons of their schoolgirl days. Through their membership in sodalities, these women tried to imitate conventual values of purity, piety, and self-sacrifice. But the spiritual guidance they received from nuns and priests ignored their new roles as wives and mothers.

Homilies to the sodalists recognized Mary as the model of true womanhood and extolled her virginity and spotlessness. In 1888 the priest-director of the St. Louis Children of Mary described the Blessed Mother's purity and holiness from the day of her conception. He implored his listeners to ask her for the grace to preserve them from all worldly passions and prejudices.[50] A few years later the ladies were reminded of the reparation they owed to the Virgin Mary for the indignities she suffered, especially in recent attacks on her virginity in the English press.[51] The Clifton Children of Mary were advised to imitate Mary in every respect, especially her humility and purity.[52] Although their audience was composed of homemakers, the directors failed to discuss Mary's role as mother and wife. Only two sermons to the St. Louis Children of Mary in fifty-five years even mentioned the family. An 1896 talk noted that the Holy Ghost animated the love of a husband and wife and helped raise children while a 1903 sermon instructed the women to model their family on the family of Nazareth.[53]

Delineating the obligations of a Catholic gentlewoman was more important than acknowledging the realities of marriage and motherhood. The same virtues of self-sacrifice, humility, submission, obedience, silence, and purity which were urged upon them as schoolgirls reappeared in sermon after sermon. Even though academy graduates belonging to sodalities chose traditional roles and held convent school values, sodality directors continued to worry that the sodalists might abandon their duties. A Cincinnati priest in 1898 inveighed against women turning toward a "worldly career" and demanded that a Child of Mary become a valiant woman, making "beautiful and happy the home circle."[54] By 1900 the director warned that women were becoming degenerate, which threatened the foundations of society.

> Purity, piety, self-sacrifice, if these are taken from her, homes are broken up and children are raised without piety or religion. If woman is untrue to herself and her God-given mission, God help us! The devil with his mighty force is against her: it is she who must save men. . . . What is the result when she forgets herself, when she abandons her mission and casts aside her virginity? When she turns to the theatre, and the so-called ambitions of life. The stories of doctors and lawyers show that a wonderful and deplorable change is coming over women. She is imitating men in gambling and drinking.[55]

Along with imploring women to be pure, pious, and self-sacrificing, the sodalities encouraged their members to engage in traditional kinds of Catholic charity work. These women rarely joined their Protestant sisters in the voluntary associations and reform movements which swept American society in the late nineteenth and early twentieth centuries.[56] Sodality ladies undertook only those activities which were approved and encouraged by their church and these did not include social reform.[57] They sewed for the poor, cared for churches, and made altar linens and vestments.

In St. Louis, where the Children of Mary increased in size from 154 members in 1876 to 303 in 1906, sodalists visited the female hospital, taught in Sunday schools and helped the blind and deaf. A St. Louis Child of Mary founded the Queen's Daughters, an organization that set up sewing and industrial schools in order to teach poor children cooking and household skills.[58] The Children of Mary also established a summer recreation camp for slum children. In 1910 these women began work in the tubercular hospital outside St. Louis, where they provided companionship for lonely patients and supplied them with gifts of fruit, candies, and books. Motivated by a concern for the spiritual needs of the inmates, the Children of Mary secured the services of a Franciscan priest for the hospital. Through the efforts of the sodalists, hundreds were baptized, a sizeable number of patients converted to Catholicism and many marriages were rectified. Moreover, the sodalists secured places in Catholic orphanages and schools for children of tubercular patients. By 1920 the Children of Mary had compiled an impressive record of Catholic charity work. With a membership of 544 women, the Children of Mary was the largest and most socially prominent Catholic sodality in St. Louis.[59]

The Chicago Children of Mary also undertook numerous social projects. Their most famous work had its beginning in 1898 at a retreat at the Taylor Street Convent. After hearing sermons on hell, death, and judgment, the sodalists expected the customary sermon on heaven. Instead, the Jesuit director preached on Christ's admonition that "it is easier for a camel to pass through the eye of a needle, than for a rich man to enter the kingdom of heaven." According to the priest's homily on Matthew's gospel, the rich man was kept from eternal happiness because of his failure in stewardship, not because of his wealth. Fired by the words of the homilist, the Children of Mary decided to found a Sunday school in the Italian slum surrounding the Sacred Heart Academy. Supported by the Sacred Heart graduates and their daughters who worked there, Guardian Angels Sunday School became the largest of its kind in the world. By 1913 it had developed into a Catholic social settlement center.[60]

Like other Catholic groups in the late nineteenth and early twentieth centuries, sodalists operated within the framework of a traditional Catholic charity work. They did not question the inequities in social, political and economic institutions and accepted Jesus' prediction that the poor would always be with them. The Children of Mary in Chicago, for example, taught Sunday school just one block south of Hull House, the nation's pioneer social settlement, founded by Jane Addams and Ellen Gates Starr in 1889. Although Addams did not abandon her original purpose of bringing beauty and culture to immigrants on Chicago's West Side, she soon turned her attention to the more immediate needs of slumdwellers. Over the years, the staff at Hull House supported trade union organizers, investigated unsanitary living and working conditions and advocated child labor laws.[61] In contrast, the Sacred Heart alumnae who established Guardian Angels Sunday School concerned themselves mostly with the spiritual needs of Italian children. Especially alarming to the Children of Mary was the large number of Italian immigrants who exchanged vows at City Hall, rather than in a Catholic church. Constrained by traditional ideas of Catholic charity work, the Children of Mary expended most of their energies in regularizing religious practices of Italian immigrants on Chicago's West Side.

The Children of Mary in St. Louis also placed the spiritual welfare of the poor above their bodily wants. In a Children of Mary "Report of Good Works, 1907 to 1908," every story reflected concern for the individual's soul. A Child of Mary wrote about her discovery of a pretty young woman in the "colored consumptive ward" in a St. Louis hospital. As a child the sick woman had been a Catholic, but later she renounced her faith and led a "dissipated" life. At first, the patient refused any assistance from the Child of Mary. After numerous acts of kindness by the sodalist, the woman consented to see a priest, who heard her confession and gave her Holy Communion. According to the Child of Mary, she died a "perfectly peaceful death" in the hospital.[62] For a sodality member, no story could have had a happier ending.

Sodalities allowed married women to recreate the atmosphere of convent life. At a time when parochial life offered women few opportunities for service, sodalities also encouraged charity work outside the home. These activities gave the members a sense of accomplishment and worth as well as providing valuable help to those in need. Yet far from challenging traditional Catholic values, sodalities did not deviate from the conventual ideal. The sodalists' overriding concern for the salvation of the people they assisted mirrored the nuns' hopes for their pupils. Not only did the sermons at sodality meetings replicate those of schoolgirl days, but they pretended to address women without husbands or children.

Furthermore, retreats afforded sodality members the opportunity to live like nuns for a few days each year. Both meetings and retreats affirmed a female world where men were neither needed or wanted.

For many academy graduates, neither marriage nor motherhood dulled their adulation of conventual life. This admiration of the nun was reflected in the poem, "To Our Second Mothers."

> You virgin spouses of a virgin King,
>   You black-robed habitants of cloistered halls,
> What endless canticles your hearts must sing,
>   What sweet Te Deums rise behind those walls.
> We who have tasted bitter with life's sweet,
>   We worldings torn with ceaseless worldly strife.
> How wondrous seem the pathways where your feet
>   Treat the still measure of a holy life.
> You chose to wear your Savior's Crown of thorns,
>   And roses blossomed and each thorn defied;
> You chose to bear the cross that you might live
>   And sought the burden that the world scorns,
> Followed the footsteps of the Crucified
>   And found the peace the world can never give.[63]

Paradoxically, even as sodalities offered married women opportunities to perform charity work outside the home, they often portrayed conventual life as more noble than matrimony. Not surprisingly, many academy graduates hoped that their children would embrace religious life as nuns, brothers, or priests. Indeed, alumnae notes and meetings often mentioned the fortunate mothers whose children had become first class members of the Roman Catholic Church.

The Single Woman

Many of the same circumstances which fostered religious vocations also encouraged academy girls to remain unmarried. Though the sisters and the clergy disapproved of the single woman, their glorification of virginity with its implied contempt for sex, and their failure to present a positive idea of marriage probably influenced many girls without a religious vocation to shun wedlock.[64]

Although they rejected religious life and marriage for

careers as teachers and office workers, the majority of unmarried academy graduates still clung to conventional ideals. For the most part, these women chose occupations that did not threaten their piety or gentility. Teaching was especially popular because it most closely resembled the work of nuns and mothers. In 1910, *The Young Eagle* called attention to this phenomenon when it asked its readers, "Who can explain the strong attraction teaching has for the convent school graduate."[65] Writing was also an acceptable occupation for the academy graduate since a woman could write at home and avoid the dangers of the workplace. However, to pursue their careers, writers often needed leisure time and money, requisites easier for the Sacred Heart graduates than for graduates of the other academies to meet.[66]

Because few convent academies included vocational courses before the turn of the century, many of the graduates were forced to seek additional training before entering the work force. As a result of changes in the curriculum after 1900, however, alumnae were better prepared for careers as teachers, secretaries, and social workers. At the beginning of the twentieth century, large numbers of convent school graduates were attracted to the relatively new occupation of social work. This career also closely resembled that of nuns and homemakers and was therefore considered appropriate for Catholic women.

Only a few convent school graduates chose careers outside office work, teaching, and social work. A St. Clara alumna, Adelaide O'Brien of St. Louis, received a law degree in 1911 and later represented the Cherokee nation before the Supreme Court. Ethel Harrington, a 1904 graduate from St. Clara, received degrees from the University of Chicago and Rush Medical School. In the same class was Caroline Gleason, a University of Minnesota and Chicago School of Civics and Philanthropy graduate who became the State of Oregon's Secretary of Commerce in 1913, the individual primarily responsible for the passage of Oregon's minimum wage law.[67] Alumnae from Mt. St. Joseph and St. Xavier also worked in professions other than traditional female ones. A

1901 graduate of Mt. St. Joseph became a journalist and another received a law degree from Cornell University while a 1915 class member took a Ph.D. in zoology from the University of Iowa.[68] Sacred Heart graduates who worked chose the same kinds of professions as the graduates of the other convent schools. Annette C. Washburne was president of Chicago's Junior League when she decided to become a doctor. After witnessing a surgical operation, she returned to school, graduating from DePaul University in 1925 and University of Illinois Medical College in 1929. Mary Agnes Amberg, a daughter of a very wealthy and prominent Chicago family, chose social work and headed the Madonna Center, a Catholic settlement center, from 1914 until 1962.[69]

Unmarried academy alumnae, like Caroline Gleason and Mary Agnes Amberg, rejected convent school expectations because they failed to enter the convent or marry. Yet they subscribed to conventual values in other ways. Instead of sacrificing themselves to God or husband and children, they denied themselves in order to help others.

The Nun

The high number of convent schoolgirls who chose a life of poverty, chastity, and obedience presents no surprise given the extraordinary religious atmosphere of the convent, the active encouragement of religious vocations by the sisters, and the esteem in which the nuns were held. Most convent schoolgirls considered this option at one time, and probably few with any inclination toward religious life could have resisted the allure of entering.

Convent schoolgirls chose religious life for a variety of psychological, social, and religious reasons. Ideally, the desire to seek spiritual perfection and serve others was their primary motivation. More likely, given that the age of entry was generally between sixteen and twenty, the girls' association with the sisters probably played the central role in such a decision. The girls observed the nuns in the intimate setting of the academy and saw many of them leading happy, productive, and fulfilled lives. Those girls who chose such a life found the world of the nuns more appealing and promising than the world of their mothers and sisters.

Along with the example of their teachers, other factors influenced the girls. The convent school environment was anti-male and to a lesser extent anti-family. Its prohibition against contact with boys, the total absence of married role models, and prolonged separation from family members must have led many girls to fear marriage. Not only did romantic attachments to fellow students and teachers make some girls reluctant to leave the protected world of the academy but they also reinforced the idea that women had no need for intellectual or emotional sustenance from men. Religious life provided a praiseworthy and socially acceptable solution to these problems.

The convent also gave aggressive and ambitious pupils an opportunity to exercise intellectual, artistic, and administrative talents, which might have remained untapped if those girls had married. Nuns earned doctorates; headed grammar schools, high schools, academies, colleges, and hospitals. They exercised real power in their own sphere with little male interference. No other women in America so fully controlled their own destinies or lived in a world so radically separate from men as did the nuns. The convent provided an extraordinary alternative for those dissatisfied with the options available to women in outside society and might partially explain the absence of middle-class Catholic women in reform movements. Many of those Catholic women who might have worked for progressive causes and led other Catholic women to join them became presidents of Catholic colleges, mother generals of their orders, college professors, hospital administrators, and school principals. The Catholic Church in America greatly benefitted from the women's choice of religious life, but it drained the laity of many of its most talented, aggressive, and ambitious women.

The Dissenters

Academy graduates for the most part lived in accordance with the lessons learned in school. Even those who remained single generally adhered to the virgin ideal and chose careers approved by the nuns. However, a few graduates rejected convent school expectations and held very different values from those of the nuns who had taught them. Unfortunately, with the exception of the occasional comment in the student register, academies and alumnae associations kept no records of their dissenters.[70] The writings of two renowned convent school alumnae, however, indicate the nature of the problems some women had with the academy ethic. These writers were Agnes Repplier and Kate Chopin.

Agnes Repplier

Agnes Repplier (1855-1942) attended the academy of the Sacred Heart in Philadelphia where she was expelled for rebelliousness. Half-seriously, she would often say that learning to smoke was one of her major accomplishments at the convent.[71] A celebrated and prolific essayist, this former academy girl often wrote about women. Her opinions sharply differed from the nuns, the clergy, and the Catholic press.

Repplier disliked the convent school portrait of the ideal woman. She attached no particular merit to the so-called feminine virtues, nor did she believe that women inherently possessed them. She did not see woman as a pure, ethereal, pious, and submissive being, who must be sheltered from the vagaries of life. Instead, Repplier saw her as a flesh-and-blood creature, neither inferior nor superior to man. She railed against chivalrous and sentimental attitudes toward women, calling chivalry protective and rooted in the consciousness of superior strength. Chivalry, she wrote,

> . . . will not assure to women a fair field and no favours, which is the salvation of all humanity; but it will protect them from the consequences of their own deeds, and that way lies perdition.[72]

The essayist believed that male adulation of women was a hypocritical attitude, one primarily responsible for the extraordinary complacency of American women. Repplier demanded equal rights for women and insisted that women accept equal obligations. She maintained that women

> . . . are neither the "gateway to hell," as Tertullian pointed out, nor the builders of Sir Rabindranath Tagore's "spiritual civilization." They are neither the repositories of wisdom, nor the final word of folly.[73]

The author's disdain for the idealization of women matched her feelings about the unfair criticisms hurled at women throughout the ages. In an 1897 essay Repplier defended the "new woman" who so disturbed the Catholic clergy. She pointed out that the "new woman" was not very new at all and that the principles urged by feminists in the late nineteenth century had been demanded by women hundreds of years before. According to Repplier, it mattered little whether "woman" fit the description of "new" or "traditional" because men had criticized her since creation for whatever course of action or inaction she took.

> Always either too new or too old, too intelligent or too stupid, too restless after what concerns her not, or too passively content with narrow aims or outlooks, she is sure to be in the wrong whether she mounts her ass or leads him.[74]

The essayist then humorously noted that in every generation only the great-grandmother satisfied male criteria for perfect womanhood. Contemporary women should be pleased to know that someday they too will be regarded as the last example of distinctly feminine traits and praised for their sewing, silence, lack of learning, and "stayathomeativeness," the quality which one male writer declared to be the "finest and rarest attribute of the sex."[75]

Repplier dismissed as nonsense the belief that home was the natural sphere of woman and homemaker her appointed role. Throughout her long writing career, Repplier pleaded for the right of women to enter any field for which they were qualified. At the end of the nineteenth century she wrote that

> Since Adam delved and Eve span, life for all of us has been full of labor; but as the sons of Adam no longer exclusively 'delve,' so the daughters of Eve no longer exclusively spin. In fact, delving and spinning, though admirable occupations, do not represent the sum total of earthly needs. There are so many, many other useful things to do, and women's eager fingertips burn to essay them all.[76]

Even after women gained the vote, Repplier saw how difficult it was for them to make their way in the professions, the trades, and politics. Rejecting the concept of feminine privilege or duties, she asked only for equal opportunity.

Repplier's belief in the capacity of women to choose their own careers extended to their choice of marital status. As a single woman, she asserted the right to remain unmarried and attacked the convent-school view that a woman must become either a nun or a homemaker. In a 1904 essay entitled "The Spinster," Repplier explained that the convent gave Catholic Christianity a practical solution to the problem of the unmated woman as well as dignity to her maidenhood.

> Bride of the Church, she did not rank as a spinster, and her position had the advantage of being accurately defined; she was part of a recognized social and ecclesiastical system. No one feels this more solidly than does a nun to-day, and no one looks with more contempt upon unmarried women in the world. In her eyes there are but two vocations—wifehood and consecrated virginity. She perceives that the wife and the religious are transmitters of the world's traditions; while the spinster is an anomaly, with no inherited background to give repute and distinction to her role.[77]

Repplier's support and praise of the single woman contrasted sharply with views held by the Catholic press, nuns, and the clergy. She noted in an 1892 essay that the three best female writers of the time, Jane Austen, Maria Edgeworth and Mary Mitford, were typical old maids, "women whose lives were rounded and completed without that element which we are taught to believe is the mainspring and prime motor of existence."[78] She mocked the view of the spinster as a pitiful, rejected, spiteful, envious, uncharitable, and ridiculous figure, who became acceptable only if she sacrificed herself for others. Repplier asked:

> What if, holding her life in her two hands, and knowing it to be her only real possession, she disposes of it in the way she feels will give her most content, swimming smoothly in the stream of her own nature, and clearly aware that happiness lies in the development of her individual tastes and acquirements?[79]

Far from apologizing, Repplier wrote that the American woman remained unmarried because she felt herself too valuable to be entrusted to a husband. Tongue-in-cheek, she inquired:

Would it be possible for any sane and thoughtful woman who was not an American to consider even the remote possibility of our spinsters becoming a detached class, who shall form "the intellectual and economic élite of the sex, leaving marriage and maternity to the less developed woman?"[80]

Repplier's praise of the single woman did not detract from her admiration of marriage when it placed the welfare and happiness of the woman on an equal level with that of the man. She insisted that matrimony must never be a duty for those who did not want to become nuns. "Marriage is a delightful thing; but it is not, and never can be, a duty; nor is it as a duty that men and women have hitherto zealously practised it."[81]

From her description of wedlock as a delightful thing to her condemnation of the idealization of woman, Repplier contradicted the convent school's expectations and image of a Catholic woman. The author praised the "new woman," upheld feminist claims, debunked the myth of separate spheres for women and enthusiastically supported the unmarried female. Whether a woman married or remained single, she must set her own goals and try to fulfill them. This kind of female bore little resemblance to the silent, obedient, home-loving, self-sacrificing woman who embraced the teachings of her church and her convent school.

Kate Chopin

Kate Chopin, née O'Flaherty (1851-1904), attended a Sacred Heart academy in St. Louis from the age of six to seventeen. She wedded Oscar Chopin in 1870, bore six children, and enjoyed a very happy marriage until her husband's death in 1883. She was well known and respected for her stories about Creole and local life in Louisiana—especially those collected in *Bayou Folk* (1894) and *A Light in Acadie* (1897)—but her novel *The Awakening* (1899) was nationally condemned for its indecent and scandalous subject matter.[82]

Like Agnes Repplier, Chopin rebelled against convent-school expectations and ideals. The St. Louis-born author sharply criticized the life of nuns instead of idealizing them. She supported women who placed their careers ahead of marriage and demanded an equal partnership between husband and wife. Abandoning proverbial convent-school modesty, Chopin frankly discussed sexuality and adultery. Her novel *The Awakening* has been described as the most important piece of fiction about the sexual life of a woman writer to date in America.[83]

Although her closest friend became a nun, Chopin saw little value in religious life. After visiting another schoolmate who entered the convent, Chopin commented in her diary:

> When we came away, my friend who had gone with me said: "Would you not give anything to have her vocation and happy life!" There was a long beaten path spreading before us . . . [where] a little dog was trotting. . . . "I would rather be that dog," I answered her. I know she was disgusted and took it for irreverence and I did not take the trouble to explain that this was a little picture of life and that what we had left was a phantasmagoria.[84]

In her short story, "Lilacs," Chopin painted an unflattering portrait of nuns who discover that a former pupil has a lover. Not only did the sisters fail to forgive her but they refused to allow her to make her annual retreat at the convent.

Marriage and motherhood, the honorable alternatives to religious life, also came under fire in Chopin's stories. Like Repplier, she challenged the idea that matrimony superseded a woman's decision for a career. In her story "Wiser Than a God," Paula, a talented and determined young musician, refused the man she loved in order to become a concert pianist. Her music was "something dearer than life, than riches, even than love."[85] She held fast to her decision even when her suitor reminded her that it was her duty to him, to God, and to herself to marry him.[86] Chopin did not oppose the institution of marriage but only unions that confined the woman and took no account of her desires or needs. In "A Point At Issue," the author approvingly described a marriage between equals.

> Marriage was to be a form, that while fixing legally their relation to each other, was in no wise to touch the individuality of either; that was to be preserved intact. Each was to remain a free integral of humanity, responsible to no dominating exactions of so-called marriage laws.[87]

Although it was written nearly a hundred years ago, the story portrayed a newly married young woman who studied French for a year in Paris while her husband taught mathematics at an American university.

Central to the author's discussion of marriage was the demand for a woman's self-determination and the rejection of the convent school model who lived only for others and thought nothing of herself. This theme appeared in "The Story of an Hour," when a wife was told that her husband had died in a railroad accident. At first she was grief-stricken, but as she sat alone in her room, she began to gain strength.

> When she abandoned herself, a little whispered word escaped her slightly parted lips. She said it over and over under her breath: "free, free, free!" . . . But she saw beyond that bitter moment a long procession of years to come that would belong to her absolutely. And she opened and spread her arms out to them in welcome.
>
> There would be no one to live for her during these coming years; she would live for herself. There would be no powerful will bending hers in the blind persistence with which men and women believe they have a right to impose a private will upon a fellow-creature. . . . She breathed a quick prayer that life might be long. It was only yesterday she had thought with a shudder that life might be long.[88]

When her husband returns home an hour later, the woman dies instantaneously. The doctors said "she had died of heart disease—of joy that kills."[89] An even stronger assertion of a woman's need for independence occurred in Chopin's famous novel, *The Awakening*. Edna Pontellier, a twenty-nine-year-old mother of two children and wife of a prosperous New Orleans businessman, falls in love with a young man and has an affair with another. The heroine realizes that her sexual desires can be separated from love and satisfied by someone she does not love. Even more shocking, the heroine feels no remorse. She disregards her duties as wife and mother and resents her children as "antagonists who . . . sought to drag her into the soul's slavery for the rest of her days."[90] At the same time Edna knows that her freedom could never be exercised in New Orleans society. She could not be the "mother woman," one of those "who idolized their children, worshipped their husbands, and esteemed it a holy privilege to efface themselves as individuals and grow wings as ministering angels."[91] Therefore, her only choice remained suicide. Chopin failed to condemn this character, who repudiated the sacred role of mother and wife, harbored strong sexual desires, committed adultery, and took her own life. However reprehensible these sins were to Victorian America, they were inconceivable in the convent-school world.

After *The Awakening*, Chopin moved even further from the convent school ethic. Unlike Edna, her characters in later stories do not suffer for their sexual desires. In "Vocation and a Voice," the hero tries to decide between his love for a woman and for God. He enters a monastery but continues to dream of the woman until one day while working outdoors he vividly remembers the sight of her when she was naked. Suddenly, he hears the voice of his beloved as she passed by his monastery.

> He watched her as she passed. He sprang upon the bit of wall he had built and stood there, the breeze lashing his black frock. He was conscious of nothing in the world but the voice that was calling him and the cry of his own being that responded. Brother Ludovic bounded down from the wall and followed the voice of the woman.[92]

Very different from the virgin martyrs and the saints of the academy, Chopin's hero rejected the call of religion for that of the flesh. Instead of suffering from qualms of conscience, he only experienced happiness. An even more radical story entitled "The Storm," concerned the adultery of a man and woman who had been sweethearts before each had married another. Chopin wrote about the sexual act in a way that was taboo among American writers.[93]

> When he touched her breasts they gave themselves up in quivering ecstasy, inviting his lips. Her mouth was a fountain of delight. And when he possessed her, they seemed to swoon together at the very borderland of life's mystery.[94]

She neither approved nor condemned their passionate lovemaking but only described how well the woman treated her husband and son that evening and how the man wrote a loving letter to his vacationing wife. The story ended with a comment about the happiness of the absent wife.

> And the first free breath since her marriage seemed to restore the pleasant liberty of her maiden days. Devoted as she was to her husband, their intimate conjugal life was something which she was more than willing to forego for a while.
> So the storm passed and every one was happy.[95]

Chopin's frank acknowledgement of female sexuality is most startling when measured against her convent-school background. It also distinguishes her from other feminist writers of the 1890s, such as Charlotte Perkins Gilman and Mary Wilkins Freeman. Chopin may have been more forthright than Agnes Repplier, yet the two women agreed that a woman must be free to choose a career and lifestyle that was not dictated by the expectations of nuns, clergy, or society in general—an opinion not held by other Catholic female writers in their era.

Conclusion

Throughout the nineteenth and early twentieth centuries, American convent schools educated young women to become nuns or homemakers. Although the majority of academy graduates married and a large number entered religious life, many remained single. Yet like their classmates who became nuns or wives, most single women adhered to conventual values. Indeed, few academy graduates strayed beyond the limits of the convent-school world or challenged traditional church teachings on the role of women. A 1916 holy picture souvenir of an adult sodality retreat described the ideal which convent-school graduates strove toward. Jesus crucified adorned one side of the card while the other asked why the saints were saints.

> Because they were cheerful when it was difficult to be cheerful, patient when it was difficult to be patient; because they pushed on when they wanted to stand still; they kept silent when they wanted to talk, they were agreeable when they wanted to be

disagreeable. That was all. It was quite simple and always will be.[96]

For most alumnae, the equation of eternal happiness with conformity to convent-school values made the price of rebellion too high.

Conclusion

*P*rotected and hidden from life outside the gates of the convent school, the Catholic academy girl learned how she must think, act, pray, and feel, if she hoped to enter heaven. She lived in a closed and ordered world where a girl could know with certainty her place in this life and the next. The teachers of the convent schoolgirl cared little about her future worldly happiness or success but wished only that she lead a life consistent with academy values and purposes. A Sister of Mercy expressed these hopes for a graduate of St. Xavier Academy in 1880.

> What wishes shall I form for thee
> > Dear child?
> Say shall I pray thy path to be
> > A sunny, thornless, rose-strewn way?
> Or shall I wish that wealth and fame
> > Thy footsteps ever may pursue?
> And friendships' sweet and sacred flame
> > May burn for Thee in radiance true?
>
> Ah better, brighter, holier things
> > May gracious Heaven to Thee impart.
> The joy approving conscience brings,
> > The peace that dwells in a spotless heart,

A life of pure and holy Love,
   Untainted by the world's decay.
And then in joys supreme above
   To bask in God's eternal day.[1]

Leaving the convent school meant contact with the "world's decay" and if marriage were chosen, it also meant the loss of a "spotless heart." Some academy girls avoided both dangers by taking the veil. Others compromised by rejecting marriage and embracing a worldly career. Whether religious, single, or married, the nuns had succeeded in forming women whose memories of the lessons learned in convent school seemed never to grow dim and whose loyalty to the church seemed never to waver.

Although the sisters and their former students rarely questioned male authority in the church, in the home, or in the workplace, they managed to construct a separate female world for the ostensible purpose of spiritual sustenance and church work. In convents, sodalities, alumnae associations and other religious organizations, these women assumed leadership positions and exercised talents without need or desire for male intrusion. While remaining perfectly faithful to the church, they transcended the roles assigned them and looked to each other for support and affirmation. At a far deeper level than their politically active Protestant counterparts who formed women's rights groups and backed female suffrage, many Catholic women thoroughly yet unintentionally rejected male domination by choosing to live in an all-female society. Nuns provided their female co-religionists with examples of productive, happy lives without the benefit of husbands and family.

Apart from the creation of a separate female world, the convent school highlighted and mirrored the weaknesses of Roman Catholicism in America during the later nineteenth and early twentieth centuries. Like the institutional church, the academy functioned as a ghetto, suspicious and fearful of the outside world and committed to safeguarding its members from contaminating influences and people. Furthermore, the intensity and isolation of the convent school added a new dimension to the church's expression of religious sentiment, glorification of virginity, ambivalence to the family, authoritarianism, and sacrifice of intellect to piety.

The effects of this convent-school education were not confined merely to two generations of Midwestern Catholic women who attended these academies. Tens of thousands of Catholics throughout the country received a schooling identical to the one described in this work. In addition, convent-school graduates carried the values they learned from the nuns to the wider Catholic community. They became sisters who staffed parochial grammar and high schools, popular writers who published for a Catholic audience, and lay teachers and social settlement workers who taught and helped in public and private institutions. Most importantly, married alumnae brought the ideals of the convent school into the home and instilled them in their children.

Few institutions in the American Catholic Church can rival the far-reaching influence of the convent school. Whatever their weaknesses or strengths, the nuns and the women educated in these schools played a crucial role in the development of a Roman Catholic faith and piety in an American setting.

Appendix

Supplementary Data

TABLE 8

Catholic Colleges and Boys Enrolled, 1860–1915

	1860	1865	1870	1875	1880	1885	1890	1895	1900	1905	1910	1915
CHICAGO												
Colleges	1	1	2	2	2	2	4	2	6	8	8	
Number in Colleges					345	480	527	680	1035	1716	1726	
CINCINNATI												
Colleges	3	4		3	3	3	3	5	5	4	5	4
Number in Colleges				724	450	500	655	955	837	1000	902	889
DUBUQUE												
Colleges	3	0	0	1	1	1		1	1	1	1	1
Number in Colleges						75			100	175	264	276
DAVENPORT												
Colleges	2	1	1	1	1	1	1					
Number in Colleges				100	100	177	225					
ST. LOUIS												
Colleges	2	2	2	4	4	4	2	3	4	1	1	2
Number in Colleges					807	760	735	786	947	520	502	595

SOURCE: *Catholic Directories*, 1860–1920.

NOTE: As noted before, figures from the *Catholic Directories* are not completely reliable. They are more approximate than exact. However, they do point to the fact that many more Catholic girls than boys received a Catholic secondary education.

TABLE 9

Number of Students Attending the Academies Under Study, 1860–1920

	1860	1865	1870	1875	1880	1885	1890	1895	1900	1905	1910	1915	1920
St. Joseph Academy (Dubuque)			100	125	120	140	200	140	140	286	477	480	390
Mt. St. Joseph (Dubuque)						90	100	120		290	185	207	230
Immaculate Conception (Davenport)			300	100	200	200	160	130	100	136	150	205	275
St. Clara (Sinsinawa)				95	95	96	100	100	142	245	220	160	215
Sacred Heart (Madison)				65	80	180	30	65	58	80		120	145
St. Xavier (Chicago)		80	210	264	221	259	247	264	212	438	491	540	895
St. Agatha (Chicago)		40						160	100				
Academy of the Sacred Heart (Chgo/Lake Forest)	36		135	125	150	150	130	145	75	90	116	100	
Academy of the Sacred Heart: City House (St. Louis)			140	140	60	65	65	50	108	150	215	204	239

continued on next page

TABLE 9 Continued

Number of Students Attending the Academies Under Study, 1860–1920

	1860	1865	1870	1875	1880	1885	1890	1895	1900	1905	1910	1915	1920
Academy of the Sacred Heart: Maryville (St. Louis)					80	115	115	115	75	135	107	74	85
Academy of the Sacred Heart: Clifton (Cincinnati)						47	50	60	65	70	75	75	95

SOURCE: *Catholic Directories*, 1860–1920.

NOTE: St. Joseph Academy (called St. Mary's Academy for three years) began in Dubuque in 1843. Mt. St. Joseph Academy opened in 1881 as the boarding school for St. Joseph Academy. St. Xavier Academy underwent a large expansion after 1904 when a new institution was built and the school moved. St. Agatha opened in 1854 and closed ten years later because the property which the bishop of Chicago, James Duggan, had ordered transferred to the Sisters of St. Joseph. It reopened in 1889. The Academy of the Sacred Heart, City House, became a day school after the boarding school at Maryville opened in 1872. All of these institutions under study, with the exception of City House after 1872, St. Joseph's after 1881, and St. Xavier's after 1904, functioned primarily as boarding schools. Yet, day students attended and their numbers are included in the above figures since most institutions listed boarders and day pupils together. Probably, about twenty to forty percent of the girls were day students. However, at the academies of the Sacred Heart, day students were completely segregated from the boarders and no contact allowed until the twentieth century.

TABLE 10

Ages of Students at the Academy of the Sacred Heart, Chicago and Lake Forest, 1858–1920

Years	6	7	8	9	10	11	12	13	14	15	16	17	18	19	20	21	22	Total	Median
1858–1870		1		3	2	1	6	5	6	9	4	9	4	3	2		2	57	15
1871–1880	1	1	2	3	3	2	3		10	4	8	4	2	3	1			47	14
1881–1890				1	2	4	5	8	3	10	5	4	8		2			52	15
1891–1900	3			1	3	4	5	5	9	5	5	4	2	2				51	14
1901–1904	3	5	2	1	4	5	6	7	8	4	1	1	2	1		1	1	48	12
1904–1910							2	2	1	13	5	9	6	6	3			46	17
1911–1920	2	2	2	2	3	4	5	8	10	16	6	5	1	2	1			66	14

SOURCE: The Student Register of the Academy of the Sacred Heart at Taylor Street, Chicago and Lake Forest, 1858–1920, Archives of the Academy of the Sacred Heart, Lake Forest.

NOTE: A random sample of students was taken for the years 1858–1870; 1871–1880; 1881–1890; 1891–1900; 1901–1904; 1904–1910 and 1911–1920. The same students were used in Tables 10, 11, and 12. Total figures vary in the tables because data was not complete for every student used in this sample. For example, a pupil counted in Table 11 might not be included in Table 10 because her birth date was missing. Since the Academy of the Sacred Heart moved from Taylor Street in Chicago to Lake Forest in 1904, the first decade of the twentieth century in these tables was divided into two periods, 1901–1904 and 1904–1910.

TABLE 11

Residences of Students at the Academy of Sacred Heart, Chicago and Lake Forest, 1858–1920

	Chicago	Illinois and Neighboring States	Other States	Foreign Countries	Total Number of Students
1858–1870	40	24	2	1	67
1871–1880	26	15	6		47
1881–1890	31	15	6		52
1891–1900	33	14	4		51
1901–1904	46	0	4		50
1904–1910	30	12	4		46
1911–1920	45	8	4		57

SOURCE: The Student Register of the Academy of the Sacred Heart at Taylor Street, Chicago, and Lake Forest.

TABLE 12

Years Spent at the Sacred Heart Academy, Chicago and Lake Forest

	Under 1 Year	1	2	3	4	5	6	7	8	9	10	11	12	Over 12	Number of Students	Median Number of Years
1858–1870	14	34	9	4	3	1	1						1		66	1
1871–1880	7	14	7	1	2	1	1	1							34	1
1881–1890	13	22	8	3											46	1
1891–1900	2	17	13	1	6	1	2	1	3	1					47	2
1901–1904	8	13	12	5		2	2	1					1		45	2
1904–1910	0	24	8	7	4	2								1	45	1
1911–1920	7	17	12	9	7	6	4	2	4	1	1			1	70	2

SOURCE: The Student Register of the Academy of the Sacred Heart at Taylor Street, Chicago, and Lake Forest.

TABLE 13

Courses Given at Various Academies under Study

St. Clara Academy, 1867–1909 Course of Studies

	1st year	*2nd year*	*3rd year*	*4th year*
1867	Christian Doctrine Grammar Composition Mental and Modern Arithmetic Ancient and Modern History	Christian Doctrine English Higher Arithmetic Algebra Geometry Bookkeeping Ancient History Latin French Philosophy	Christian Doctrine Rhetoric Geometry Astronomy Latin French Philosophy	Christian Doctrine Miscellaneous Writing Botany Physiology Chemistry Latin French Domestic Economy Intellectual Philosophy
1881	Christian Doctrine Orthography Composition Elocution Literature Bookkeeping Higher Arithmetic Physical Geography Latin Natural Philosophy	Christian Doctrine Orthography Composition Literature Higher Arithmetic Algebra U.S. History Ancient History Astronomy Geology Latin French (optional)	Christian Doctrine Orthography Composition Literature Elocution Geometry Algebra Ancient History Modern History Physiology Latin French (optional)	Christian Doctrine Elocution Orthography Penmanship Composition Trigonometry Geometry Chemistry Intellectual Philosophy

St. Clara Academy *continued*

1901

Ancient Classical

1st year	2nd year	3rd year	4th year
Christian Doctrine	Baltimore Catechism	Wilmer's Handbook of Christian Doctrine	Wilmer's Handbook of Christian Doctrine
English	English	English	English
Algebra	Plane Geometry	Solid Geom.	Review of Math
History of Greece & Rome	Medieval History	Const. Hist.	Review of Hist. of Art (weekly)
Latin	Latin	Modern Hist.	Latin
	Greek	Hist. of Art (weekly)	Greek
		Greek	Logic
		Latin	

English Scientific

1st year	2nd year	3rd year	4th year
Christian Doctrine	Baltimore Catechism	Wilmer's Handbook	Wilmer's Handbook
English	English	English	English
Algebra	Plane Geometry	Solid Geometry	Review of Math.
History of Greece & Rome	Medieval History	Const. Hist.	Review of Hist. of Art (weekly)
Botany	Physics	Modern Hist.	Rev. Sci.
Physics	French or German	Hist. of Art (weekly)	French or German
French or German		Astronomy	Logic
		Chemistry	
		French or German	

Modern Classical

1st year	2nd year	3rd year	4th year
Christian Doctrine	Baltimore Catechism	Wilmer's Handbook	Wilmer's Handbook
English	English	English	English
Algebra	Plane Geometry	Solid Geometry	Review of Math.
History of Greece & Rome	Medieval History		

TABLE 13 Continued

St. Clara Academy *continued*

Modern Classical

1st year	2nd year	3rd year	4th year
French or German	French or German	Const. Hist.	Review of Hist. of Art (weekly)
Latin	Latin	Modern Hist.	Latin
		Hist. of Art (weekly)	French or German
		French or German	Logic
		Latin	

Classical

1909	1st year	2nd year	3rd year	4th year
	Religion	Religion	Religion	Religion
	English	English	English	English
	Algebra	Plane and Solid Geom.	Medieval & Mod. History	Adv. Algebra
	Civics	2d Foreign Language	2d Foreign Lang.	Solid Geometry
	Hist. of Greece & Rome		Drawing	Amer. History
	Foreign Language			Geography
				Physics
				Foreign Lang.

Scientific

1st year	2nd year	3rd year	4th year
Religion	Religion	Religion	Religion
English	English	English	English
Algebra	Plane and Solid Geom.	Medieval & Mod. History	Adv. Algebra
Civics	Science	Science	Amer. History
History of Greece & Rome	Foreign Language	Foreign Language	Physics
Science		Drawing	Foreign Language
			Drawing

St. Xavier Academy, 1873–1904 Course of Studies

	1st year	2nd year	3rd year	4th year
1873	Christian Doctrine Reading Spelling Penmanship Practical/Mental Arithmetic Sacred History Physical Geography Familiar Science	Christian Doctrine Grammar Composition Literature Practical/Mental Arithmetic Sacred History Physical Geography Familiar Science	Christian Doctrine Reading Penmanship Rhetoric Algebra Geometry Natural History Geology Chemistry Physiology Botany Philosophy	Christian Doctrine Composition Penmanship Rhetoric Bookkeeping Geometry Natural History Geology Chemistry Physiology Botany Philosophy
1883	Christian Doctrine—Deharbe's Catechism Reading Writing—Rhetoric Etymology Practical/Mental Arithmetic General History Physical Geography Familiar Science French & German (optional) Music Drawing	Christian Doctrine—Deharbe's Catechism Reading Writing—Rhetoric Etymology Arithmetic Algebra General History Physiology French & German (optional) Music Drawing	Christian Doctrine—Deharbe's Catechism Reading Writing—Epistolary Correspondence Literature—Rhetoric Composition Algebra Bookkeeping Civil Government General History Review Botany French & German (opt.) Music Drawing	Christian Doctrine—Deharbe's Catechism Writing Epistolary Composition Mythology Geometry Trigonometry Astronomy—Zoology Chemistry—Geology Natural Philosophy French, German, Latin (optional) Music Drawing

TABLE 13 Continued

St. Xavier Academy continued

	1st year	2nd year	3rd year	4th year

1894	Faith of Our Fathers
	Reading—Literature
	Composition—Rhetoric
	Writing—Grammar
	Algebra
	Arithmetic
	General History
	Physiology
	French, German, or Latin
	Music
	Drawing
		Faith of our Fathers
		Reading
		Writing—Rhetoric
		Composition—Literature
		Arithmetic
		Algebra
		General History
		Physiography
		French, German, Latin,
		  or Greek
		Music
		Drawing
			Church History
			Reading—Mythology
			Writing—Composition
			Literature
			Epistolary Correspondence
			Geometry
			Zoology
			Physics
			French, German, Latin,
			  or Greek
			Music
			Drawing
				Church History
				Writing
				Epistolary Correspondence
				Reading
				Trigonometry
				Astronomy
				Geology
				Chemistry
				French, German, Latin,
				  or Greek
				Psychology
				Music
				Drawing

1904	Religion
	English
	Reading
	Algebra
	Greek and Roman History
	Physiology/Physiography
	Latin
	French, German, Italian
	  —electives
		Religion
		English
		Reading
		Algebra
		Medieval and Modern
		  History
		Zoology
		Latin
		French, German, Italian
		  —electives
			Religion
			English
			Geometry
			English History
			Physics
			Latin
			French, German, Italian
			  —electives
				Religion
				English
				U.S. History
				Astronomy
				Chemistry
				Latin
				French, German, Italian
				  —electives
				Psychology

Sacred Heart Academies' Course of Studies, 1879–1917

	1st year	2nd year	3rd year	4th year
1879	Catechism, Gospel Church History Grammar—Orthography Composition—Reading Mental & Practical 　Arithmetic American History Geography French Reading & German	Catechism, Gospel Church History Composition—Etymology Grammar—Orthography Mythology Mental & Practical 　Arithmetic American History Geography French Reading, German 　Conversation, 　Translation, 　Orthography Natural Philosophy	Catechism—Church 　History Gospel—Maxims/Proverbs Composition—Epistolary 　Style Etymology Algebra & Mental 　Arithmetic Ancient and Medieval 　History Botany Astronomy French Reading, 　Conversation, 　Translation, Grammar, 　Orthography, History Logic	Catechism—Proverbs Gospel Composition History of Literature Epistolary Style Mental & Practical 　Arithmetic Bookkeeping Modern European History Physics—Mineralogy 　(1 quarter each) Chemistry—Physiology 　(1 quarter each) French Classics Psychology
1899	New Testament Bible & Church History Grammar Ancient Literature Classics Arithmetic Ancient History Geography	New Testament History of English 　Language English Literature Classics Algebra English History Physics	New Testament Church History Rhetoric Classics Medieval Literature Algebra General History—to 1453 Geography	New Testament Literature—English & 　Foreign Masterpieces Classics Plane Geometry General History 1453– 　1789 Mineralogy

TABLE 13 Continued

Sacred Heart Academies *continued*

	1st year	2nd year	3rd year	4th year
	Lessons in Physiography & Botany French Latin	French Latin Logic	Astronomy Latin French Psychology	Elements of Chemistry Latin French Ethics Ontology
1917	New Testament Christian Doctrine Composition Classics Algebra Sacred History Physiography French Latin	New Testament Christian Doctrine Bible History Composition Ancient Literature Classics Algebra (1 semester) Ancient History Botany (1 semester) French Latin	New Testament Christian Doctrine Church History Composition English Literature Classics Plane Geometry American History English History Latin French Logic	New Testament Christian Doctrine Church History Composition Medieval Literature Classics Algebra, Geometry, Trigonometry (elective) Universal History Chemistry (elective) Latin French Psychology

BVM Academies' Course of Studies, 1883–1910

St. Francis—

	1st year	2nd year	3rd year	4th year
1883	Christian Doctrine	Christian Doctrine Orthography	Christian Doctrine Composition	Christian Doctrine Literature

	1st year	2nd year	3rd year	4th year
		Elocution	Rhetoric	Rhetoric
		Rhetoric	Penmanship	Geometry
		Epistolary	Elocution	History
		Correspondence	Algebra	Astronomy
		Algebra	History	Geology
		History	Botany	Botany
		Physical Geography	Zoology	Natural Philosophy
		Familiar Science		

Mt. St. Joseph's—

1891	Catechism of	Church History	Church History	Church History
	Perseverance	Composition	Composition	Composition
	Composition	Rhetoric	Reading	English Authors
	Grammar	Reading	Ancient Literature	Geometry
	Rhetoric—Reading	Literature	Geometry	Chemistry
	Arithmetic	Prose/Poetry	General Review	Astronomy
	Bookkeeping (optional)	Algebra	of Studies	Geology
	Algebra	Ancient History	French or German	French or German
	Modern History	Botany	Philosophy	Logic
	Zoology	French or German		
	French or German			

English Classical

1902	Christian Doctrine	Christian Doctrine	Christian Doctrine	Spalding's Church History
	Rhetoric	Composition	Rhetoric	Essay Writing
	Composition	Rhetoric	Composition	Critical Study
	Literature	Literature	Critical Study	English Lit.
	Critical Study	Critical Study	Solid Geometry	English History (elective)
	Algebra	Plane Geometry	Latin	Astronomy (elective)

TABLE 13 Continued

Mt. St. Joseph's *continued*

1st year	2nd year	3rd year	4th year
History of Greece & Rome	History of Mod. Nations	Greek or French or German	Latin
Biology	Physics		Greek or French or German
Latin	Latin		Logic
French or German	Greek or French or German		

English Scientific

1st year	2nd year	3rd year	4th year
Christian Doctrine	Christian Doctrine	Christian Doctrine	Spalding's Church History
Rhetoric	Composition	Rhetoric	Essay Writing
Composition	Rhetoric	Composition	Critical Study
Literature	Literature	Critical Study	English Lit.
Critical Study	Critical Study	Solid Geometry	English History (elective)
Algebra	Plane Geometry	Chemistry	Astronomy
History of Greece & Rome	History of Mod. Nations	Geology	Latin or French or German
Biology	Economics	Latin or French or German	
Latin or French or German	Physics		
	Latin		
	French or German		

Immaculate Conception—			
1st year	2nd year	3rd year	4th year

	1st year	2nd year	3rd year	4th year
1910	Religion	Catechism of	Catechism of	Christian Philosophy
	English (American Authors)	Perseverance	Perseverance	English
	Algebra	Church History	History of Persecution,	Solid Geometry
	History	Reading	Councils	Chemistry
	Latin	English	Middle Ages, Heresies,	Geology
		Algebra	Liturgies	Astronomy
		Medieval & Reformation	English	Latin
		History	Plane Geometry	
		Botany	Civil Government	
		Latin	Physics	
			Latin	

SOURCE: St. Clara Academy Catalogues, 1867, 1881, 1902, 1909, APO. St. Xavier Academy Catalogues, 1873, 1883, 1894, 1904, ASM. St. Francis Academy Catalogue, 1883; Mt. St. Joseph Academy Catalogues, 1891, 1902; Immaculate Conception Academy Catalogues, 1910, ABVM. Louise Callan, *The Society of the Sacred Heart in North America*, pp. 756–59, 763–65; Plan of Studies for the Academy of Sacred Heart, Maryville, St. Louis, 1917–1918, ARSCJ.

TABLE 14

Public High School Education in Chicago, 1861

Synopsis of the General Course

	First Term	Second Term	Third Term
1	Algebra German or Latin Descriptive Geography	Algebra German or Latin Eng. Grammar & Analysis	German or Latin Physical Geography
2	Algebra German or Latin Universal History	Geometry German or Latin Universal History	Geometry German or Latin Universal History Botany
3	Geometry German, Latin, or French Physiology Rhetoric	Trigonometry German, Latin, or French Natural Philosophy English Literature	Mensuration Navigation and Surveying German, Latin, or French Natural Philosophy English Literature
4	Astronomy German, Latin, or French Intellectual Philosophy Constitution of United States Bookkeeping	Chemistry German, Latin, or French Logic Political Economy	Geology and Mineralogy German, Latin, or French Moral Science Political Economy

Reading during the first and second years. Drawing during the second, third, and fourth years. Composition and declamation throughout the entire course.

Synopsis of the Classical Course

1	Algebra Harkness' *First Latin Book* Descriptive Geography	Algebra Harkness' *First Latin Book* English Grammar and Analysis	Arithmetic Latin Reader Physical Geography
2	Algebra Latin Reader Universal History	Geometry Caesar Universal History	Geometry Caesar Universal History Botany
3	Greek Caesar or Cicero Physiology	Greek Cicero Natural Philosophy	Greek, *Anabasis* Cicero Natural Philosophy
4	Greek, *Anabasis* Virgil, *Eclogues* Cicero Latin Prose	Greek Virgil, *Aeneid and Georgics* Latin Prose	Greek, *Iliad* Virgil, *Aeneid* Review of Latin

Reading during the first and second years. Drawing, the second, third, and fourth years. Composition and declamation during the entire course. Classical antiquities, military affairs, during the second year. Classical antiquities, civil affairs, during the third year. Classical antiquities, mythology, during the fourth year.

SOURCE: Marion Talbot, *The Education of Women*, (Chicago: The University of Chicago Press, 1910), pp. 95–96.

TABLE 15

Cincinnati, Ohio, 1872

Grade D

First Session		Second Session	
Latin	History, 4	Latin	History 4,
College Latin	Composition, 1	College Latin	Composition, 1
German	Elocution, 1	German	Elocution, 1
Algebra	Drawing, 1	Algebra	Freehand Drawing, 1
Anatomy, Physiology & Hygiene, 2		Anatomy, Physiology Hygiene, 2	

Grade C

First Session		Second Session	
Latin	Algebra, 4	Latin	English Grammar, 4
College Latin	History, 4	College Latin	Composition, 1
Greek	Composition, 1	Greek	Elocution, 1
French	Elocution, 1	French	Freehand Drawing, 1
German	Freehand Drawing, 1	German	

Grade B

First Session		Second Session	
Latin	English Literature, 3	Greek	Botany, 3
College Latin	Natural Philosophy, 4	French, 4	English Literature, 3
Grek	Elocution, 1	German, 4	Composition, 1
French, 4	Drawing, 1	Geometry and Plane & Spherical Trigonometry	Elocution, 1
German, 4	Latin, 4	Natural Philosophy, 4	Drawing, 1
Geometry	College Latin		

Grade A	
First Session	*Second Session*
Latin, 3	Latin, 3
College Latin	College Latin
Greek	Greek
French, 3	French, 3
Astronomy, completed, 4	Plane Surveying, 3
Chemistry, 4	Chemistry, 4
Natural History, 1	
Mental Philosophy, 1	Mental Philosophy, 1
Constitution of U.S., 1	Geology, 3
Bookkeeping, 2	Natural History, 1
English Literature, 3	English Literature, 3
Composition, 1	Composition, 1
Drawing, 1	Drawing, 1

Pupils in the Grades A, B, and C may, under the direction of the principal, select from the studies of their respective grades an amount of work equal to fifteen recitations per week exclusive of Composition, Reading, and Declamation. In the latter branch all pupils shall have one lesson every two weeks.

SOURCE: John Elbert Stout, *The Development of High-School Curriculum in the North Central States from 1860 to 1918*. (Chicago: The University of Chicago, 1921), pp. 21–22.

TABLE 16

St. Louis, Missouri, 1881

First year	Second year	Third year	Fourth year
Latin	Algebra	Greek or Bookkeeping or	History of English Literature
Arithmetic	Natural Philosophy	Mechanical Drawing	Shakespeare and Constitu-
Physiology or German	Latin	Latin or German or French	tion of United States
Rhetoricals 3	German or Greek	General History	Latin or French or German
Drawing 2	History of Art or Mechanical	Chemistry 2	Zoology and Geology or
	Drawing	Rhetoricals 3	Greek or Laboratory
	Rhetoricals 3	Geometry 2	Chemistry or Mental
	Drawing 2		Philosophy or
			Trigonometry
			Rhetoricals 2

The boys in the Senior class are required to take 2 of the 6 studies under 4. Music throughout the course.

SOURCE: John Elbert Stout, *The Development of High-School Curriculum in the North Central States from 1860 to 1918.* (Chicago: The University of Chicago, 1921), p. 29.

TABLE 17

Milwaukee, Wisconsin, 1884

English–Science Course

	First Term	Second Term	Third Term
First Year	Algebra Grammar and Composition Etymology	Algebra Grammar and Composition Etymology	Algebra Arithmetic Physiology
Second Year	Geometry General History Biology	Geometry General History Biology	Trigonometry General History Rhetoric
Third Year	Physics English History English Literature	Physics English Literature United States Constitution	Physics Physiology Political Economy
Fourth Year	Chemistry Astronomy English Classics	Chemistry Mental Science English Classics	Geology Mental Science American Classics

Theme writing throughout the last three years. German or French elective for English History or Political Science in the third year, or for Mental Science and Astronomy in the fourth year.

TABLE 17 Continued

Milwaukee, Wisconsin, 1884

German–English Course

First Year	Substitute German for Etymology, Latin, and Physiology.
Second Year	Substitute German for General History.
Third Year	Substitute German for English History, United States Constitution, and Political Economy.

Fourth Year	Chemistry	Geology
	English History	Political Economy
	German	German
	Civil & Literary History	Civil and Literary History

General History elective for mathematics in the second year.

Latin–English Course

	First Term	*Second Term*	*Third Term*
First Year	Algebra	Algebra	Algebra
	English Composition	English Grammar	Physiology
	Latin Grammar	Latin Lessons	Latin Grammar Lessons
Second Year	Geometry	Geometry	Trigonometry
	Biology	Biology	Rhetoric
	Caesar	Caesar	Cicero
Third Year	Physics	Physics	Physics
	English Literature	English Literature	Physiology
	Cicero	Cicero	Virgil
Fourth Year	English History	Civil Government	Roman History
	English Classics	English Classics	Two elective studies
	Virgil	Eclogues	

German or French elective for English Literature, Physiology, and English Classics of the third and fourth years for those desiring to prepare for College.

SOURCE: John Elbert Stout, *The Development of High-School Curriculum in the North Central States from 1860 to 1918.* (Chicago: The University of Chicago, 1921), pp. 29–30.

TABLE 18

Chicago, Illinois, 1894

Six Years' College Preparatory Course

Sixth Class—First Year	Latin, 5 English, 4 Arithmetic and Geometry, 4 American History, 4	Penmanship and Drawing, 2 Physiology and Hygiene, 1 German, 1
Fifth Class—Second Year	Latin, 5 English, 4 Algebra and Geometry, 4	English & American History, 3 Drawing, 2 German or French, 2
Fourth Class—Third Year	Latin, 4 English, 4 Algebra and Geometry, 4 until March, 1 Arithmetic with applications of Geometry, 4; after March, 1	Botany, 4, ½ year Elements of Chemistry, 4, ½ year Drawing, 2
Third Class—Fourth Year	Latin, 4 English including Mythology, 4 French or German, 2	Greek, 3 Plane Geometry, 4 Drawing, 2 Elements of Geology, 1
Second Class—Fifth Year	Latin, 4 English, 2 Greek, 4 French or German, 2	Grecian and Roman History, 4 Plane Trigonometry and Review Algebra, 4 Drawing, 1
First Class—Sixth Year	Latin, 5 French or German, 2 Greek, 4 English, 2	English, German, French, and American History, 3 Physics, 4

SOURCE: John Elbert Stout, *The Development of High-School Curriculum in the North Central States from 1860 to 1918.* (Chicago: The University of Chicago, 1921), p. 36.

TABLE 19

Chicago High Schools Course of Study, 1909

Subject	First Year		Second Year		Third Year		Fourth Year	
	No. of Recitations per Week	No. of Weeks	No. of Recitations per Week	No. of Weeks	No. of Recitations per Week	No. of Weeks	No. of Recitations per Week	No. of Weeks
English	4	40	4	40	4	40	4	40
Latin	4	40	5	40	5	40	5	40
German	4	40	5	40	5	40	5	40
French	4	40	5	40	5	40	5	40
Spanish	4	40	5	40	5	40	5	40
Greek			4	40	4	40	4	40
Mathematics	4	40	4	40				
Physiography	6	30						
Physiology	4	10						
Accounting	6	40	6	40				
Biology			6	40				
Stenography & typewriting			6	40	6	40	4	20
Civics							4	40
History			4	40	8	40	6	40
Physics or Chem.					6	40		
Commercial Geography					4	40		
Geology							4	20
Astronomy							4	20
Commercial law							4	20
Economics							2	20
Drawing	2	40	2	40	2	40	1	40
Music	1	40	1	40	1	40	1	40
Physical culture	1	40	1	40	1	40		
Domestic science & arts	6	50	6	50	6	50	6	50

SOURCE: Marion Talbot, *The Education of Women* (Chicago: The University of Chicago Press, 1910), p. 103.

NOTE: For graduation the requirements were three and one-half consecutive years of English; two consecutive years of some foreign language; two consecutive semesters of mathematics; four semesters of science; and two semesters of history. Marion Talbot, *The Education of Women*, pp. 103 –104.

TABLE 20

Marriage Rates of the General Female Population, 1890–1920

		1890	1900	1910	1920
25 to 29	Married	71.36	68.9	71.8	73.4
	Single	25.38	27.5	24.9	23.0
30 to 34	Married	79.76	78.0	79.0	80.1
	Single	15.16	16.6	16.1	14.9
35 to 44	Married	80.64	79.5	80.1	80.3
	Single	9.8	11.1	11.4	11.4

SOURCE: U.S. Department of Commerce, Bureau of the Census, *Eleventh Census of the United States, 1890: Compendium*, p. 117; *Twelfth Census of the United States, 1900: Abstract*, p. 22; *Thirteenth Census of the United States, 1910: Abstract*, p. 149 and *Fourteenth Census of the United States, 1920: Population*, 2:390.

Abbreviations
used in notes

ARSCJ   National Archives of the Society of the Sacred Heart in America, St. Louis, Missouri

ASM   Archives of the Sisters of Mercy of Chicago, Chicago, Illinois

ABVM   Archives of the Sisters of Charity of the Blessed Virgin Mary, Dubuque, Iowa

AOP   Archives of the Sinsinawa Dominicans, Sinsinawa, Wisconsin

Notes

1. In order to avoid confusion, the terms nuns, sisters, and religious will be used interchangeably in this book to refer to vowed Catholic women belonging to Catholic religious orders. Technically, "nuns" should be used to designate women professed of solemn or simple vows, temporary or perpetual, in a monastery in which solemn vows are taken and at least minor papal cloister is observed. "Sisters" take simple vows, temporary or perpetual, in a religious congregation. They are bound by common or episcopal cloister which is much less stringent than that observed by "nuns" and gives them opportunities for apostolic work. *New Catholic Encyclopedia*, 1967 ed., s.v., "Nuns," and "Sisters." The Sisters of Mercy, the Sisters of Charity of the Blessed Virgin Mary and the Sinsinawa Dominicans, three of the four orders treated in this study, were sisters. The members of the fourth order, the Society of the Sacred Heart, were called "religious" because at the time the Society gained official approval (1826), Rome did not give complete legal recognition to "sisters." The Society of the Sacred Heart substituted a vow of stability for papal enclosure, which made them neither second order nuns nor third order sisters. Like the other three groups, the Society of the Sacred Heart will be described as sisters, nuns, or religious in this work.

2. The number of public high schools in America increased rapidly after 1865. In 1870 there were at least 160. Ten years later 800

existed. By 1890 there were 2,526 and in 1900, 6,005. In 1910 the number increased to 10,213 and in 1920, 14,326. The number of girls attending public high schools in 1890 was 116,351 while those in private high schools and academies totalled 47,397. By 1910, 516,536 went to secondary public schools and 61,926 received their education in private institutions. Thomas Woody, *A History of Women's Education in the United States*, 2 vols. (New York: The Science Press, 1929), 1:545-46. Unfortunately, no comprehensive study of girls' private secondary education after 1870 exists. However, the education of girls in public high schools and colleges and universities has been treated in a number of historical works.

Chapter 1: Background

1. Woody, 1:21. See also, Ann Ewing Hickey, *Women of the Senatoreal Aristocracy of Late Rome as Christian Monastics* (Ann Arbor, Mi.: U.M.I. Research Press, 1986).

2. Joan M. Ferrante, "The Education of Women in the Middle Ages in Theory, Fact and Fantasy," in *Beyond Their Sex: Learned Women of the European Past*, ed. Patricia H. Labalme (New York: New York University Press, 1980), p. 13.

3. Ibid., p. 14.

4. Eileen Power, "The Position of Women," in *The Legacy of the Middle Ages*, ed. C. G. Crump and E. F. Jacobs (Oxford: Clarendon Press, 1926), p. 413. See also, Angela M. Lucas, *Women in the Middle Ages* (New York: St. Martin's Press, 1983), pp. 137-56.

5. Suzanne F. Wemple, *Women in Frankish Society: Marriage and the Cloister, 500 to 900*, (Philadelphia: University of Pennsylvania Press, 1981), p. 176.

6. Eileen Power, *Medieval English Nunneries*, (Cambridge: Cambridge University Press, 1922; reprint edition, New York: Bilbo & Tannen, 1964), pp. 261-78.

7. Jo Ann Hoeppner Moran, *The Growth of English Schools 1340-1548* (New Jersey: Princeton University Press, 1985), p. 116.

8. Ferrante, "Education of Women in the Middle Ages," in Labalme, *Beyond Their Sex*, p. 12.

9. Power, *Medieval English Nunneries*, p. 238.

10. Ferrante, "Education of Women in the Middle Ages," in Labalme, *Beyond Their Sex*, p. 23.

11. Margaret L. King, "Book-Lined Cells: Women and Humanism in the Early Italian Renaissance," in Labalme, *Beyond Their Sex*, p. 68.

12. Ibid., pp. 75-80.

13. Foster Watson, ed. *Vives and the Renascence Education of Women* (London: Edward Arnold, 1912), p. 24.

14. William H. Woodward, *Studies in Education During the Age of the Renaissance, 1400-1600* (New York: Russell & Russell, 1965), p. 209.

15. Sister Mary Monica, *Angela Merici and Her Teaching Idea, 1474-1540* (New York: Longmans, Green & Co., 1927), p. 303.

16. Ibid., p. 302.

17. H. C. Barnard, *Madame de Maintenon and Saint-Cyr* (London: A. & C. Black, LTD, 1934), p. 43.

18. Sister Mary Monica, *Angela Merici*, p. 374.

19. Mother Mary Margarita O'Connor, *That Incomparable Woman* (Montreal: Palm Publishers, 1962), p. 65.

20. James R. Cain, *The Influence of the Cloister on the Apostolate of Congregations of Religious Women* (Rome: Pontifical University, 1965), p. 47.

21. Archbishop François Fénelon, "Advice from M. De Fénelon, Archbishop of Cambrai, to a Lady of Quality, concerning the Education of her Daughter," *Fénelon on Education*, ed. H. C. Barnard (Cambridge, England: University Press, 1966), p. 98.

22. Fénelon, "The Education of Girls" in *Fénelon on Education*, ed. Barnard, p. 75.

23. Ibid., pp. 75-90.

24. Barnard, ed. *Fénelon on Education*, p. xxxv.

25. Barnard, *Madame de Maintenon and Saint-Cyr*, p. 227.

26. Ibid., pp. 173-79.

27. Ibid., pp. 197-98.

28. Woody, 1:330.

29. Mother Mary Benedict Murphy, "Pioneer Roman Catholic Girls' Academies: Their Growth, Character and Contribution to American Education" (Ph.D. dissertation, Columbia University, 1958), p. 39.

30. Annabelle M. Melville, *Elizabeth Bayley Seton 1774–1821* (New York: Charles Scribner's Sons, 1951), pp. 213-14.

31. Sister Helen Louise Nugent, *Sister Louise: Josephine van der Schrieck, 1813–1886, American Foundress of the Notre Dame de Namur.* (New York: Benziger Bros., 1931), p. 196.

32. Ibid., p. 210.

33. *The United States Catholic Almanac or Laity's Directory* (Baltimore: James Myres, 1836), p. 137.

34. Academies, also known as seminaries, educated girls between the ages of twelve and nineteen. They provided most of the secondary education available to American girls from 1775 to 1870.

35. Ann F. Scott, "The Ever Widening Circle: The Diffusion of Feminist Values from the Troy Female Seminary, 1822-1872," *History of Education Quarterly* 19 (Spring 1979):3-25; and Nancy Cott, *The Bonds of Womanhood* (New Haven: Yale University Press, 1977), p. 119.

36. Elizabeth A. Green, *Mary Lyon and Mount Holyoke* (New Hampshire: University Press of New England, 1979), p. 65.

37. Ibid., p. 341.

38. Woody, 1:326.

39. Kathryn Kish Sklar, *Catherine Beecher: A Study in American Domesticity* (New Haven: Yale University Press, 1973), p. xiii.

40. *Life and Life-Work of Mother Theodore Guerin* (New York: Benziger Bros., 1904), p. 447.

Chapter 2: The Religious Orders

1. Mary Ewens, *The Role of the Nun in Nineteenth Century America* (New York: Arno Press, 1978), p. 37.

2. Roger Aubert discusses the phenomenal growth of European religious orders in the nineteenth century. In France the number of male religious was 25,000 and female 37,000 in 1789. By 1877 the number reached 30,387 for the men and 127,753 for the women. *The Church in a Secularized Society* (London: Darton, Longmans & Todd, 1978), p. 113.

3. Outside of the academy, secondary education for Catholic girls began with high schools attached to parish schools, followed by central high schools. In the Archdiocese of Chicago, the Sisters of Mercy established high schools for girls in the parishes of St. James (1890), St. Elizabeth (1890) and St. Gabriel's (1895). The B.V.M.'s opened St. Mary's High School in 1899, the first central

Catholic high school for girls in the United States. In 1918 the Sinsinawa Dominicans founded a non-parish affiliated high school, Trinity High School. The Mercies opened their central high school in 1924. Sister Mary Innocenta Montay, "The History of Catholic Secondary Education in the Archdiocese of Chicago" (Ph.D. dissertation, Catholic University of America, 1952).

4. A description of a Catholic academy in an 1890 history of Kansas, shows one of the important functions of a sisters' school in a frontier area.

> "The Lady Superior, Sister Stanislaus, is one of the cultured ladies the State of New York sends us. . . . One of the finest musicians in the West gives instruction in that department. All the higher branches are taught. . . . Young ladies go from here prepared to enter and adorn society." John Letham, *Historical and Descriptive Review of Kansas*, 2 vols. (Topeka: n.p., 1890) 1:188-89, quoted in Sister Mary Evangeline Thomas, *Footsteps on the Frontier: A History of the Sisters of St. Joseph, Concordia, Kansas* (Maryland: Newman Press, 1948), p. 166.

5. Kathryn Kish Sklar described Catherine Beecher's development of the ideology of domesticity as an effort to gain lost status for women by assigning them the central place in the home and the family. *Catherine Beecher: A Study in American Domesticity* (New Haven: Yale University Press, 1973). Ann Douglas, in *The Feminization of American Culture* (New York: Knopf, 1977), discusses a "feminine disestablishment" in mid-nineteenth-century America when women's labor and function in society were not as visible as in earlier periods.

6. Jay Dolan analyzes the evangelism that swept the American Catholic Church in the second half of the nineteenth century in his book *Catholic Revivalism: The American Experience, 1830-1900* (Notre Dame: University of Notre Dame Press, 1978).

7. *The Rule of St. Augustine and the Constitutions of the Sisters of Penance of the Third Order of St. Dominic* (n.p., 1889), p. 22.

8. Ibid., pp. 95-96.

9. Ibid., p. 111.

10. Religious orders believed that an exclusive friendship between two sisters would separate them from the rest of the community and possibly arouse jealousy and resentment. They also feared the development of homosexual liaisons between close friends. In her study of a lesbian nun in Renaissance Italy, Judith C. Brown quoted St. Augustine's warning to his sister, who had taken holy

vows: "The love which you bear one another ought not to be carnal but spiritual: for those things which are practiced by immodest women, even with other females, in shameful jesting and playing, ought not to be done even by married women or by girls who are about to marry, much less by widows or chaste virgins dedicated by a holy vow to be handmaidens of Christ." Brown also notes that from the thirteenth century on, monastic rules required nuns to stay out of each other's cells, to leave their doors unlocked so that superiors could check on them and to avoid special friendships. Judith C. Brown, *Immodest Acts* (New York: Oxford University Press, 1986), p. 8.

11. *Rule and Constitutions of the Religious Sisters of Mercy* (Philadelphia: H. L. Kilner & Co., 1890), p. 43.

12. M. Jane Coogan, B.V.M., *The Price of Our Heritage*, 2 vols. (Dubuque: Mt. Carmel Press, 1975), 1:222.

13. Janet Erskine Stuart, "Conferences on Education," undated notes on Stuart's conferences to the Religious of the Sacred Heart, ARSCJ.

14. Sister Samuel, "One of Many," undated reminiscences of Sister Samuel, AOP.

15. Margaret Williams, R.S.C.J., *Saint Madeleine Sophie: Her Life and Letters* (New York: Herder & Herder, 1965), pp. 13, 14, 31, 44.

16. Louise Callan, R.S.C.J., *The Society of the Sacred Heart in North America* (London: Longmans, Green & Co., 1937), pp. 58-59.

17. Margaret Williams, R.S.C.J. *The Society of the Sacred Heart: History of a Spirit, 1800-1975* (London: Darton, Longmans & Todd, 1978), p. 73.

18. Nelson J. Callahan, ed., *The Diary of Richard L. Burtsell, Priest of New York* (New York: Arno Press, 1978), pp. 283-84.

19. E. Ten Broeck, R.S.C.J. to Father Daniel Hudson, April 6, 1890. Archives of the University of Notre Dame.

20. Roland B. Savage, S.J., *Catherine McAuley* (Dublin: M. H. Gill & Son, 1949), p. 47.

21. *Rule and Constitutions of the Religious Sisters of Mercy*, p. 3.

22. The Sisters of Mercy of Chicago encountered serious problems with Bishops Van de Velde and O'Regan over a seventeen acre plot of lakeshore property to which the Mercies and the bishops claimed ownership. Bishop O'Regan obtained the deed to the prop-

erty from the Mercies in 1856. The Mercies believed, however, the property was their own despite the transfer of deed.

23. M. Jane Coogan, B.V.M. *Mary Frances Clarke* (Dubuque: Mt. Carmel Press, 1977), p. 210.

24. Sister M. Paschala O'Connor, O.P., *Five Decades: History of the Congregation of the Most Holy Rosary* (Sinsinawa: Sinsinawa Press, 1954), p. 23.

25. Mary Routtan left the community in the company of the founder's nephew, Father Francis Mazzuchelli. She attempted to return to the Sinsinawa Dominicans but Father Samuel Mazzuchelli turned her away. Samuel Mazzuchelli, O.P. to Bishop Blanc of New Orleans, April 16, 1850, Archives of the University of Notre Dame.

26. O'Connor, *Five Decades*, p. 43.

27. Callan, *Society of the Sacred Heart in N.A.*, p. 729.

28. Williams, *The Society of the Sacred Heart*, p. 41.

29. Callan, *Society of the Sacred Heart in N.A.*, p. 727.

30. Ibid., p. 735.

31. Ibid., p. 741.

32. *Rule and Constitutions of the Religious Sisters of Mercy*, p. 5.

33. Catherine McAuley, "Spirit of the Institute," in *Letters of Catherine McAuley*, ed. Sister Mary Ignatia Neumann, R.S.M. (Baltimore: Helicon Press, 1969), p. 387.

34. Roland Savage, *Catherine McAuley*, p. 268.

35. *A Guide for the Religious Called the Sisters of Mercy* (London: St. Anne's Press, 1888), pp. 8-9.

36. "On the Schools," handwritten notes, n.d., ASM.

37. *A Guide for the Religious Called the Sisters of Mercy*, p. 13.

38. Coogan, *The Price of Our Heritage*, 1:114-15.

39. Coogan, *Mary Frances Clarke*, p. 248.

40. Ibid.

41. Ibid., p. 249.

42. Ibid., pp. 254-55.

43. *The Rule of the Third Order of St. Dominic* (New York: Sadlier & Co., 1860), p. 49.

44. Ibid., p. 51.

45. "Kenwood's Golden Jubilee—Catholic Training Schools," *Messenger of the Sacred Heart*, November 1903, p. 565.

46. Catholic bishops and educators recognized the problem of ill-educated teaching sisters. Legislation from the Third Plenary Council in 1884 recommended both diocesan examinations for prospective teachers of a diocese and religious normal schools for teacher training. Neither proposal met with success and led to a demand from Bishop John Lancaster Spalding of Peoria for normal-school training of teaching sisters. The bishop noted that a "good religious is not therefore a good teacher" and that the teacher training given during the novitiate had little value. John Lancaster Spalding, "Normal Schools for Catholics," *Catholic World*, April 1890, p. 95. James A. Burns, C.S.C., the leading American Catholic educational historian, also worried about the sisters' lack of teacher training. He believed that the comparative neglect of the formal study of pedagogy by the nuns was a serious defect and along with Spalding called for the establishment of a central normal school, which would be used by several religious orders. J. A. Burns, C.S.C., "The Training of the Teacher," *American Catholic Quarterly Review* 28 (October 1902):664-83. In 1913, Rev. J. C. Ei wrote that the theoretical and practical training of sisters has been sorely neglected at times. He recommended the institution of a definite program of pedagogy in the novitiate which would lead to a graded certificate. J. C. Ei, "Difficulties Encountered By Religious Superiors in the Professional Training of Their Teachers," *The Catholic Education Association Bulletin*, 10 (November 1913):362-79.

47. Coogan, *The Price of Our Heritage*, 2:176.

48. Sister Mary Eva McCarty, O.P., *The Sinsinawa Dominicans: Outlines of Twentieth Century Development, 1901-1949* (Dubuque: Hoermann Press, 1952), pp. 34-35; 279.

49. The Diocese of Leavenworth (1915) and the Archdiocese of Chicago (1919) demanded a high school education for new teachers in grades above the fifth. Cleveland (1928) asked for professional training for beginning teachers corresponding to that required by the state of Ohio, which was two years of training. The Archdiocese of Cincinnati (1933) wanted all new teachers to possess the archdiocesan certificate. Brooklyn (1936) insisted on all teachers finishing high school while New York (1938) required all elementary teachers to have a normal certificate or a certificate of experience which was granted to those with fifteen years of teaching.

J. A. Burns, C.S.C. and Bernard J. Kohlbrenner, *A History of Catholic Education in the United States* (New York: Benziger Brothers, 1937), pp. 225-26. State requirements were much more stringent than diocesan regulations. As of 1921, Illinois required for their four year high school certificate, graduation from a college or university, three years of experience and examinations in four subjects. For a county certificate, the state required two years in an institution of higher learning and examinations in eight subjects. Iowa demanded four years of college with the requisite subjects or examinations in twenty-seven subjects for the state certificate. Missouri's five year state certificate entailed two years at the state normal school and examinations in six subjects. Wisconsin's state license demanded graduation from a college, university or normal school with the required courses. Katherine M. Cook, *State Laws and Regulations Governing Teachers' Certification* (Washington, D.C.: Government Printing Office, 1921), pp. 39-198.

50. Mother Emily Power to the Sinsinawa Dominicans, May 31, 1903, AOP.

51. Diary of Sister M. Crescentia Markey, April 17, 1898 and June 21, 1898, ABVM.

52. Coogan, *The Price of Our Heritage*, 2:308.

53. The few university degrees held by the sisters did not deter them from establishing their own colleges. In 1901 the Sinsinawa Dominicans opened St. Clara's College in Sinsinawa. The official biographer of Mother Emily Power of Sinsinawa asked: "How could it be done by teachers who had never been to college, to say nothing of having no degrees?" Mary Synon, *Mother Emily of Sinsinawa* (Milwaukee: Bruce Publishing Co., 1955), p. 216. The B.V.M.'s opened Mt. St. Joseph College in Dubuque in 1901 while the Mercies started Xavier College in Chicago in 1912. The Society of the Sacred Heart established Barat College in Lake Forest in 1918 and Maryville College in St. Louis in 1923. All these colleges grew out of the academies under study in this work.

54. Thomas Edward Shields,, "The Sisters College," *The Catholic Educational Review* 3 (January, 1912):2.

55. Coogan, "Educating the Educators," paper delivered at the American Catholic Historical Association at the University of Notre Dame, April 1979, p. 8.

56. Mary H. Quinlan, R.S.C.J., *Mabel Digby-Janet Erskine Stuart* (n.p., Sacred Heart Higher Education Association, 1982), p. 170.

57. The Religious of the Sacred Heart in America recognized the need for university training long before the 1920s. Some of their members sat in on classes at Catholic universities in the early 1890s. However, Mabel Digby, the superior general from 1895 to 1911, halted this practice.

58. A questionnaire issued by the National Catholic Welfare Conference Bureau of Education asked female religious communities about the teacher preparation of their sisters between the years 1925 and 1930. Of the sixty-six communities replying to the questionnaire, only five had a rule prescribing pre-service training from which no exceptions were allowed. In each of the five cases the rule was made between the years 1922 and 1932. John Raphael Hagan, "The Diocesan Teachers College: A Study of Its Basic Principles," (Ph.D. dissertation, Catholic University of America, 1932), p. 19.

59. Rev. J. Elliott Ross, O.P., "Leisure for our Teaching Orders," *The Catholic School Journal* 20 (October, 1920):205.

60. Catholic teachers lagged far behind public school teachers in obtaining university degrees. Between 1890 and 1905, it has been estimated that 70% of all men teachers and 53% of all women teachers in high schools were college graduates. By 1917, 69% of the teachers in 1032 public high schools accredited by the North Central Association had college degrees. These figures do not include the large number of high school teachers who had normal school degrees. Edward A. Krug, *The Shaping of the American High School* (New York: Harper & Row, 1964), pp. 187 and 441.

61. George Sand, *My Convent Life*, trans. Maria Ellery McKay (Boston: Roberts, 1893; reprint ed., Chicago: Academy Press, 1978), p. 106.

Chapter 3: Convent School Life

1. Sacred Heart Academy Catalogue, Madison, Wisconsin, 1904-1905, AOP.

2. See the Appendix, Tables 9 through 12 for enrollment figures, ages, residences and length of stay at the academies. All the academies under study are listed in the enrollment table while only the Academy of the Sacred Heart in Chicago and later in Lake Forest is represented in the other charts. Unlike the Society of the Sacred Heart, the B.V.M.'s, the Mercies, and the Sinsinawa Domin-

icans failed to preserve their student registers which might have provided this information.

3. Plan of Studies for the Academy of the Sacred Heart, Maryville, St. Louis, 1917 and 1918, ARSCJ.

4. St. Clara Academy catalogues, 1867, 1909, AOP; and Mt. St. Joseph Academy Catalogues, 1887, 1909, ABVM.

5. St. Xavier Academy Catalogue, 1877, 1899, ASM; Prospectus for the Academy of the Sacred Heart, Clifton, 1870, ARSCJ; Ledger Book of Accounts of Students in Clifton, 1870-1899, ARSCJ; and Catalogues for the Academy of the Sacred Heart, Maryville, 1900, 1917-1918, ARSCJ.

6. Ledger Book of Accounts of Students in Clifton, 1870-1899, ARSCJ.

7. Student Account Books, City House, St. Louis, 1834-1917, ARSCJ.

8. Ibid.

9. Lula Kidder to her mother, June 30, 1898, *A Tribute Book to Genevieve Donnersberger, née Lula Kidder by Her Family* (n.p., n.d.), AOP.

10. Notebook of Sister Charles Borremeo Stevens, n.d., AOP.

11. Sister Mary St. Joan of Arc Coogan, B.V.M., "History of the Immaculate Conception Academy of Davenport, Iowa," (M.A. thesis, Catholic University, 1941), p. 61.

12. The subjects offered at the academies under study are listed in Table 13 in the Appendix.

13. Tables 14 through 19 in the Appendix provide representative courses of study for Midwestern public high schools in the period under study in this work. These schools offered a much stronger academic education than that given in the academies until the end of the nineteenth century. In the 1890s the convent schools finally began to give their students a secondary education that was comparable to that of the public high schools. This can be seen in the courses of study for Chicago public high schools in 1894 and 1909. However, the academies were still distinguished from the high schools by their emphasis on fine arts.

14. Callan, *The Society of the Sacred Heart in N.A.*, p. 741.

15. Plan of Studies for the Academy of the Sacred Heart, Maryville, 1917 and 1918, ARSCJ.

16. Test Books, St. Xavier Academy, 1891-1892, ASM.

17. St. Clara Academy Examinations, 1893, AOP.

18. St. Clara Academy Examinations, 1893, 1894, 1895, AOP; Test Books, St. Xavier Academy, 1891-1892, ASM.

19. The girls at St. Clara Academy were asked if they could "show by history that the Church is not opposed to the reading of Sacred Scripture?" "Questions Asked at the Final Examination," *The Young Eagle*, June 1891, p. 88, AOP.

20. Janet Erskine Stuart, R.S.C.J., *The Education of Catholic Girls* (London: Longmans, Green & Co., 1911), p. 60.

21. Chicago Province Vicariate Tests, 1908-1915, ARSCJ.

22. Memorial of the Visit of Reverend Mother Tucker, February 14, 1874, Taylor Street, Chicago, ARSCJ.

23. *Rule of the School and Plan of Studies of the Society of the Sacred Heart of Jesus*, trans. the Society of the Sacred Heart (Roehampton, England: The Society of the Sacred Heart, 1904), p. 114.

24. Sacred Heart Academy Catalogue, Madison, Wisconsin, 1899, AOP.

25. Final Examination Items, *The Young Eagle*, July 1884, p. 1, AOP.

26. Chicago Province Vicariate Tests, 1908-1915, ARSCJ.

27. Test Books, St. Xavier Academy, 1891-1892, ASM.

28. Chicago Province Vicariate Tests, 1908-1915, ARSCJ.

29. Williams, *St. Madeleine Sophie: Her Life and Letters*, p. 461.

30. Final Examination Items, *The Young Eagle*, July 1884, p. 1, AOP.

31. Chicago Province Vicariate Tests, 1908-1915, ARSCJ.

32. Girls educated in Catholic academies generally could not meet the requirements for university or college admission until the early twentieth century. In 1868 the University of Wisconsin required geography, arithmetic, alegebra, English, Latin, and Greek. Marion Talbot, *The Education of Women* (Chicago: The University of Chicago Press, 1910), p. 131. Vassar College demanded in 1875 Latin, algebra, geometry, geography, English, Greek or French or German. James M. Taylor and Elizabeth H. Haight, *Vassar* (New York: Oxford University Press, 1915), p. 65. The academy graduates finally were able to meet university requirements at such institu-

tions as the University of Wisconsin in 1908. The subjects demanded at Wisconsin in this year appeared in most of the convent school curriculums. Talbot, p. 135. However, non-Catholic girls' schools in many cases made provisions for instruction in classical languages in preparation for college entrance. Latin appeared in more than one-half of the non-Catholic academies between 1810 and 1870 which were surveyed by Thomas Woody in his *History of Women's Education in the United States,* and Greek was offered about half as frequently as Latin. Woody, 1:413.

33. St. Clara taught Latin in 1867 while Immaculate Conception offered it in 1876. Yet it only appeared in St. Xavier's program in 1884, at Mt. St. Joseph in 1902 and in Sacred Heart schools in 1899. None of the academies included Greek in their curriculum until 1894 and the Sacred Heart schools never offered it in this period. In 1902 St. Clara and Mt. St. Joseph finally introduced a classical program which prepared the girls for college entrance examinations.

34. Mt. St. Joseph Academy, St. Clara Academy, and St. Xavier Academy catalogues, ABVM, AOP, and ASM.

35. Plan of Studies for the Academy of the Sacred Heart, Maryville, 1917 and 1918 and Chicago Vicariate Exams, 1908-1915, ARSCJ.

36. Frederick Rudolf, *Curriculum: A History of the American Undergraduate Course of Study Since 1636* (San Francisco: Jossey-Bass, 1977), pp. 186-88, 213-14.

37. Stuart, *The Education of Catholic Girls,* pp. 116, 121.

38. *Rule of the School and Plan of Studies of the Society of the Sacred Heart of Jesus,* p. 112.

39. Ibid., p. 121.

40. *The Young Eagle,* July 1884, p. 1, AOP.

41. As noted in Chapter I, Zilpah Grant and Mary Lyons deliberately omitted the "ornamental branches" in their schools. The women's colleges founded after the Civil War also renounced the accomplishments. Thomas Woody in *A History of Women's Education in the United States* stated that music and art barely had a place in women's colleges except as electives and in some colleges did not appear at all. Woody, 2:194.

42. Mt. St. Joseph Academy, St. Clara Academy, and St. Xavier Academy catalogues, ABVM, AOP, and ASM.

43. *Rule of the School and Plan of Studies of the Society of the Sacred Heart of Jesus.*

44. Ibid.

45. By 1890 Mt. St. Joseph taught bookkeeping, typing, and shorthand. In the 1890s St. Clara and St. Xavier offered these same classes and a teacher's preparation course. The catalogue at St. Xavier listed 53 pupils who held teacher's certificates in 1890 and 105 in 1901.

46. Callan, *Society of the Sacred Heart in N.A.*, p. 761.

47. "The Woman Question," *Catholic World*, May 1869, p. 155.

48. Maurice Francis Egan, "Chats with Good Listeners," *Ave Maria*, 23 July 1892, p. 101.

49. Katharine Tynan, "The Higher Education for Catholic Girls," *Catholic World*, August 1890, pp. 616-17.

50. Dorothy E. Kimball, "The Convent School in America," *Catholic Educational Review*, March 1913, p. 264. The author does not identify the school or religious community she discussed. It is apparent though that she is writing about the Society of the Sacred Heart. This article was also one of the few published in the American secular and academic press which discussed convent school education. However, an English periodical, *Fraser's Magazine*, July 1874, pp. 778-86, published a very critical article on convent school education.

51. James A. Burns, C.S.C., *Catholic Education: A Study of Conditions* (New York: Longmans, Green & Co., 1917), pp. 115-25.

52. Ibid., p. 122.

53. John T. Murphy, "The Opportunities of Educated Catholic Women," *American Catholic Quarterly Review* 23 (July 1898):612.

54. "The Reader," *Messenger of the Sacred Heart*, March 1890, p. 230.

55. "Convent Training," *The Citizen*, n.d., quoted in *The Young Eagle*, December/January 1892, p. 19, AOP.

56. Ibid.

57. St. Xavier Academy Catalogue, 1873-74, ASM.

58. *Rule of the School and Plan of Studies of the Society of the Sacred Heart of Jesus.*

59. *The Rule of St. Augustine and the Constitutions of the Sisters of Penance of the Third Order of St. Dominic*, p. 93.

60. Student Register for the Academy of the Sacred Heart in Chicago and Lake Forest, 1858-1920. Both of the children's mothers lived in Chicago. Archives of the Academy of the Sacred Heart, Lake Forest.

61. Maryville School Journal, 1879-1925, October 1, 1905, ARSCJ.

62. Agnes Repplier, "Un Congé sans Cloche," in *In Our Convent Days* (Boston: Houghton Mifflin Company, 1905), p. 134.

63. Repplier, "The Convent Stage," pp. 42-44.

64. Ibid., p. 44.

65. My discussion of student plays in the convent school relies primarily on Repplier's essay "The Convent Stage."

66. These plays were performed at the Academies of the Sacred Heart, Lake Forest, Clifton, and Maryville; St. Agatha Academy, Chicago; Mt. Carmel Academy, Wichita; St. Xavier, ARSCJ, ABVM, and ASM.

67. Program for *The Fable of the Ugly Duckling*, drama presented at Woodlands Academy of the Sacred Heart, Lake Forest, May 9, 1914, ARSCJ.

68. Mt. St. Joseph Academy Catalogue, 1902, ABVM.

69. Immaculate Conception Academy Catalogue, 1910-1911, ABVM.

70. *St. Xavier's Echo*, March 1893, p. 28, ASM.

71. *The Maryville Comet*, 27 April 1907, ARSCJ.

72. Ibid.

73. Sports rose to prominence in America toward the end of the nineteenth century. Female students throughout America began to play organized sports in the 1880s and 1890s. Donald J. Mrozek, *Sport andAmerican Mentality 1880-1910* (Knoxville: University of Tennessee Press, 1983) and Betty Spears and Richard Swansen, *History of Sport and Physical Activity in the UnitedStates*, 2d. ed. (Dubuque: Wm. C. Brown Co., 1983).

74. *St. Xavier's Echo*, July 1891, p. 1.

75. Margaret A. O'Reilly, "Louise Imogen Guiney, Sacred Heart Girl," *The Signet*, October 1921, p. 3, ARSCJ.

76. Repplier, "The Game of Love," *Convent Days*, p. 225.

77. Repplier, "Reverend Mother's Feast," *Convent Days*, p. 212.

78. Repplier, "In Retreat," *Convent Days*, p. 75.

79. Rhoda Walker Edwards, "A Letter from a Alumna of the Nineteenth Century to her Grandchild of the Twentieth," September 10, 1953, p. 9, ARSCJ. Edwards was a pupil of the Academy of the Sacred Heart during the nineteenth century.

80. The Maryville Sacred Heart Alumna, St. Louis, 1915, ARSCJ.

81. Rhoda Walker Edwards, p. 3. See n. 79 above.

82. Mrs. Emma Trauscht, "Memories of a Student at St. Clara, 1902-1906," Oral History Collection, Sinsinawa, Wisconsin.

83. Dorothy Garesché Holland, "Maryville—The First One Hundred Years," *The Bulletin* 29 (April 1973): 145-62.

84. *Rule of the School and Plan of Studies of the Society of the Sacred Heart of Jesus*, p. 12.

85. Repplier, "The Game of Love," *Convent Days*, p. 220.

86. O'Reilly, p. 4.

87. *Pall Mall Gazette*, Maryville, St. Louis, 23 March 1906, ARSCJ.

88. *The Sesame*, St. Xavier's Academy Yearbook, 1911, ASM.

89. Ibid.

90. Carol Smith-Rosenberg discusses romantic friendships between women in her article "The Female World of Love and Ritual: Relations Between Women in Nineteenth Century America," *Signs* I (Autumn 1975): 1-29. She notes that these commonly accepted, deeply felt, same-sex friendships did not prevent the women involved from seeking marriage. See also Jane Hunter's discussion of special friendships among single American missionaries in turn-of-the-century China. Jane Hunter, *The Gospel of Gentility* (New Haven: Yale University Press, 1984), pp. 70-79 and Barbara Solomon's description of the romantic friendship among college women in the nineteenth and early twentieth centuries, *In the Company of Educated Women: A History of Women and Higher Education in America* (New Haven: Yale University Press, 1985), pp. 99-100.

1. See Ann Taves, *The Household of Faith: Roman Catholic Devotions in Mid-Nineteenth Century America* (Indiana: University of Notre Dame Press, 1986). Taves describes and analyzes the piety, practices, prayers, and devotional literature of the American church. Her work discusses the roots and significance of much of the piety found in the convent school.

2. *Rule of the School and Plan of Studies of the Society of the Sacred Heart of Jesus*, pp. 14-15; and notes on the history of St. Xavier Academy, Chicago, ASM.

3. During the second half of the nineteenth century, a number of prominent French and Italian clerics such as Dupanloup, Gerbert, Don Bosco and Don Frassenetti, advocated the frequent reception of communion. A 1905 decree of the Congregation of the Council urged the faithful to receive communion frequently.

4. Mrs. Mary Jane O'Brien Cavanaugh, Memories of the Benton school, 1856 to 1860 in "Reminiscences of Father Mazzuchelli and His Times," AOP.

5. Antonia White, *Frost in May* (New York: Dial Press, 1933), pp. 45-46.

6. Repplier, "Reverend Mother's Feast," *Convent Days*, p. 188.

7. "Maryville Boarding School Journal, 1879-1925," December 8, 1885, ARSCJ.

8. Enfant de Marie Minutes, 1870-1910, Clifton, Cincinnati, December 8, 1904, ARSCJ.

9. Maryville Boarding School Journal, 1879-1925, May 1915, ARSCJ.

10. Clifton School Journal, 1901-1946, Clifton, Cincinnati, May 1911, ARSCJ.

11. Daniel A. Lord, S.J., *Our Nuns* (New York: Benziger Brothers, 1924), p. 153.

12. E. Clinch, R.S.C.J., "Recollections of Taylor Street," ARSCJ.

13. Surveillante Generalé's Memorial, Clifton, 1920, ARSCJ.

14. Clifton School Journal, 1901-1946, Clifton, June 1911, ARSCJ.

15. Rhoda Walker Edwards, p. 13. See n. 79, ch. 3.

16. Clifton School Journal, 1901-1946, Clifton, March 2, 1902, ARSCJ.

17. Lula Kidder to her mother, March 31, 1897 and April 29, 1897, *A Tribute Book to Genevieve Donnersberger, née Lula Kidder by Her Family.*

18. Repplier, "In Retreat," *Convent Days*, p. 81.

19. White, *Frost in May*, p. 134. The graphic descriptions of hell in White and James Joyce's *Portrait of the Artist as a Young Man* are remarkably similar. Paul Johnson's *History of Christianity* (New York: Atheneum, 1977) discussed the popularity of the hell sermon in Catholic schools in the nineteenth century in which the children learned of the gruesome terrors of eternal punishment.

20. Repplier, "In Retreat," *Convent Days*, p. 82.

21. Enfant de Marie Minutes, 1870-1910, Clifton, ARSCJ.

22. Ibid., November 6, 1881.

23. Ibid., December 8, 1904.

24. Minutes of the Sodality of the Angels, 1897-1913, Clifton, March 11, 1913, ARSCJ.

25. Mt. St. Joseph Catalogues, 1890-1914; Immaculate Conception Catalogue, 1910; and St. Francis Academy, Council Bluffs, Iowa, 1895, ABVM.

26. Sister Mary Agatha O'Brien to Sister Mary Elizabeth, June 28, 1851, ASM.

27. Harriet Rose Collection, 1833-1922, Chicago Historical Society.

28. Catholic periodicals occasionally printed articles describing Protestant appreciation of convent schools. Invariably, non-Catholics were portrayed as grateful for the cultural and moral advantages that a girl could only receive in a Catholic academy. Typical of these articles was "A Non-Catholic's Appreciation," *Ave Maria*, 30 September 1911, p. 438.

29. Student Register of the Academy of the Sacred Heart, City House, St. Louis, 1840-1872, ARSCJ.

30. Student Register of the Academy of the Sacred Heart, Clifton, 1870-1898, ARSCJ.

31. Enfant de Marie, "School Days at the Sacred Heart," *Putnam's Magazine*, March 1870, p. 282.

32. Sister Charles Borromeo Stevens, O.S.D. [Carola Milanis], "The Old Wooden Cradle, " *Little Essays for Friendly Readers* (Dubuque: M. S. Hardie, 1909), p. 179.

33. Ibid., p. 184.

34. The desire of Protestant children to imitate their Catholic schoolmates in religion was reflected in the request of the non-Catholic children of the Academy of the Sacred Heart in St. Joseph, Missouri to the Superior General of the Society of the Sacred Heart for permission to join the sodality. Mother Adéle Lehon, superior general, replied to their request in 1879. She told them that she was pleased by their desire but as long as their parents did not allow them to practice Catholicism they could not belong to the sodalities because these organizations implied sacraments. She urged the children to pray, to see the truth and follow it in time so as to reach heaven. ARSCJ.

35. Maryville Boarding School Journal, 1879-1925, December 8, 1891, ARSCJ.

36. Ibid., January 22, 1888.

37. Stevens, "Another Chapter From Glad Old Times," *Little Essays*, p. 237. The author failed to provide the date and the location of this school. It appears though that the time period is probably the late 1870s or early 1880s and the city might be Madison, Wisconsin.

38. Ibid., p. 240.

39. A notebook of the library holdings of the adult Children of Mary in St. Louis gives a clear indication of what the academy girls and the graduates read. A letter of E. Mahoney, R.S.C.J. to Mother Sareus, R.S.C.J., Vicar of Canada, March 28, 1898, listed the magazines in the children's library. They were *The Century, The Catholic World, Scribner's, St. Nicholas, Littell's Living Age, Messenger of the Sacred Heart, The Chimes,* and *Ave Maria.* ARSCJ.

40. *The Young Ladies Illustrated Reader* (New York: The Catholic Publication Society, 1889), p. 386. The story of Agnes appeared in the *Messenger of the Sacred Heart,* February to May 1870; "The Child Martyr," *Ave Maria,* 20 January 1866 and Henry E. O'Keefe, "St. Agnes, A Type and a Contrast," *Catholic World,* January 1919.

41. *Messenger of the Sacred Heart,* August 1878, pp. 343-52.

42. C. Gilberton, "Blessed Martinia, Martyr," *American Catholic Quarterly Review* 38 (April 1914):288-302, and "St. Martinia, Virgin and Martyr," *Ave Maria,* 27 January 1877, pp. 54-56.

43. *Excelsior Fourth Reader* (New York: D. & J. Sadlier & Co., 1904), pp. 156-59.

44. *Messenger of the Sacred Heart*, March 1903, p. 288 and "A Heroine of the Catacombs," *Messenger of the Sacred Heart*, January 1881, pp. 1-12; February 1881, pp. 49-61; March 1881, pp. 97-107 and April 1881, pp. 145-158.

45. "Vito and Corine," *Messenger of the Sacred Heart*, April 1884, p. 150.

46. "The Story of Christine de Sainte-Vicent," *Messenger of the Sacred Heart*, February 1880, p. 101.

47. "A Wife's Sacrifice," *Messenger of the Sacred Heart*, October 1910, pp. 658-65.

48. Ruth Connolly, "Tributes to Our Blessed Lady by Non-Catholic Poets," *The Labarium*, November 1906, pp. 170-75. ABVM.

49. Zita E. Kavanaugh, "Queen of the Rosary," *The Labarium*, December 1907, p. 106.

50. Marie Bray, "Devotion to the Blessed Virgin," *The Labarium*, March 1908, p. 180.

51. Essays and Poetry from St. Clara Academy, 1895, AOP.

52. Eleanor C. Donnelly, "The Angelic Saint," *Immaculate Conception Portfolio*, June 21, 1878, ABVM.

53. Ruth Fox, "Bitter Sweet, " *The Young Eagle*, January 1913, p. 1, AOP.

54. Mabelle Claire Bredette, "Gethseme," *The Young Eagle*, April 1905, p. 58, AOP.

55. Patricia, "Domine Non Sum Dignus," St. Xavier's Echo, January 1893, p. 7.

56. Beatrice Johnson, "The Hound of Heaven," *The Labarium*, April 1909, p. 182.

57. Miriam Claire, "Vocation," *The Labarium*, February 1909, p. 1.

58. "My Spouse," *The Young Eagle*, September 1906, p. 1, AOP.

59. "Religious Reception and Profession, " *The Young Eagle*, September 1894, p. 9, AOP.

60. "Dedicated to the Chosen Twelve," *The Young Eagle*, September 1901, p. 206, AOP.

61. M.F.S., "A Novice's Reception into the Society of the Sacred Heart," *Messenger of the Sacred Heart*, June 1892, p. 463.

62. White, *Frost in May,* pp. 53-54.

63. Christa Ressmeyer Klein discussed the piety of Catholic boys in "The Jesuits and Catholic Boyhood in Nineteenth-Century New York City: A Study of St. John's College and the College of St. Francis Xavier" (Ph.D. dissertation, University of Pennsylvania, 1976). Like the sisters, the Jesuits encouraged an emotional and submissive piety. However, the Jesuits recognized that their kind of piety was unattractive to American Catholic boys and modified it by glorifying the virtues associated with athletics and the military. Klein noted that the Jesuits' introduction of competitive sports and military drill in their schools marked the New York Jesuits' advocacy of a new student ideal which combined a masculine ethos with Catholic piety.

Chapter 5: Expectations and Reality

1. John Lancaster Spalding in *Woman: A Collection of Tributes to Woman,* ed. the Sisters of Charity of the B.V.M. (Davenport, Iowa: Gorman and Son, 1893), p. 81, ABVM.

2. Sister Genevieve Granger to Kate, April 5, 1856, ASM.

3. McCarty, *Sinsinawa Dominicans,* pp. 279-81.

4. Mother Mary Isabella to the B.V.M. Sisters, March 14, 1922 and September 15, 1928, ABVM.

5. Introduction, *Woman: A Collection of Tributes to Woman,* p. 1, ABVM.

6. Nathaniel Hawthorne, in *Woman: A Collection of Tributes to Woman,* p. 23, ABVM.

7. Hannah Moore, in *Woman: A Collection of Tributes to Woman,* p. 13, ABVM.

8. Mrs. Hermas, in *Woman: A Collection of Tributes to Woman,* p. 123, ABVM.

9. Stevens, "Our Nutshell Boundaries," *Little Essays,* pp. 112-13.

10. Ibid., p. 117.

11. Sister Mary Ruth, O.S.D., "The Curriculum of the Woman's College in Relation to the Problems of Modern Life," *The Catholic Educational Review* 14 (September 1917):124.

12. See Table 8 in the Appendix for the number of boys educated in Catholic colleges.

13. Stevens, "Woman, The Homemaker, And The Effect of Her Surroundings," *Little Essays* p. 151.

14. See Colleen McDonnell, *The Christian Home in Victorian America, 1840-1900* (Bloomington: Indiana University Press, 1986). McDonnell describes Catholic attitudes toward domesticity.

15. "Mary, the True Woman," *Ave Maria*, 10 April 1869, pp. 225-28.

16. Joseph Huselein, S.J., "The Woman Question," *The Catholic Mind*, 10 December 1913, p. 356.

17. "Thoughts for the Women of the Times," *Catholic World*, January 1872, p. 470.

18. "The Woman Question," *Catholic World*, May 1869, p. 151.

19. "Woman's Place in Christian Society," *Ave Maria*, 5 October 1867, p. 629.

20. Edward E. Murphy, "What Women Wanted," *America*, 20 November 1915, p. 128.

21. Quoted in Hasia R. Diner, *Erin's Daughters in America* (Baltimore: The John Hopkins University Press, 1983), p. 151.

22. "How the Church Understands and Upholds the Rights of Woman," *Catholic World*, May 1872, p. 262.

23. Martha More Avery, "Genesis of Woman Suffrage," *America*, 16 October 1915, p. 6 and "Woman Suffrage," *The Catholic Mind*, 8 December 1915, pp. 625-55.

24. James Kenneally, "American Catholicism and Women," in *Women in American Religion*, ed. Janet Wilson James (Pennsylvania: University of Pennsylvania Press, 1980), p. 194. Elizabeth Worland Carr in her "American Catholic Woman and the Church to 1920," (Ph.D. dissertation, St. Louis University, 1982), added to this list Archbishop Patrick Riordan of San Francisco, Bishop James Keane of Cheyenne, Bishop Austin Dowling of Des Moines and Reverend John Ryan of Catholic University. Father Scully of St. Mary's, Cambridge, Mass., urged his female parishioners to vote in Cambridge's election because of his support for a "no license" ordinance that he hoped would lessen Irish drinking. Hasia R. Diner, *Erin's Daughters in America*, p. 150.

25. Cardinal James Gibbons, "Relative Condition of Woman Under Pagan and Christian Civilization," *American Catholic Quarterly Reivew* 10 (October 1886):651-65.

26. Allen Sinclair Will, *The Life of Cardinal Gibbons, Archbishop of Baltimore* (New York: E. P. Dutton & Co., 1922), pp. 783-84, quoted in Carr, pp. 135-36.

27. Archbishop John J. Glennon, Introduction to *Loretto Centennial Discourses, 1812-1912* (St. Louis: Herder, 1912), p. iv-v.

28. "Address of the Most Reverend Sebastian G. Messmer, D.D., Archbishop of Milwaukee," *The Young Eagle*, 11 July 1911, p. 149, AOP.

29. Rt. Rev. John T. McNicholas, "The Catholic Woman of Today," *The Young Eagle*, July 1919, p. 162, AOP.

30. Rev. P. J. Garrigan, Bishop of Sioux City, "Who Shall Find a Valiant Woman," *The Labarium*, June 1907, p. 63.

31. William J. Onahan, "Ideals of Christian Womanhood," *The Young Eagle*, June 1913, p. 168, AOP.

32. Rev. Charles Moulinier, S.J., "Baccalaureate Sermon," *The Young Eagle*, July 1911, p. 152, AOP.

33. "Address of Archbishop John Keane of Dubuque," *The Labarium*, July 1912, p. 275.

34. Address of Archbishop Messmer, *The Young Eagle*, 11 July 1911, p. 150, AOP.

35. Address of William J. Onahan, *The Young Eagle*, June 1913, p. 168, AOP.

36. Quoted in Barbara Solomon, *In the Company of Educated Women*, p. 49.

37. Ibid., pp. 115-40.

38. Only the writings of girls attending Sinsinawa Dominican, B.V.M. and Mercy academies appear in this section. Except for two issues of a newspaper written by Maryville girls, no writings of students from the academies of the Sacred Heart were available.

39. "Woman's Sphere," *Mt. St. Joseph Messenger*, November 1883, p. 8.

40. "What a Girl Ought to Do in the World," *The Young Eagle*, July 1884, p. 2, AOP.

41. "Our Privileges as Maidens," *St. Xavier's Echo*, June 1891, p. 47.

42. "My Ideal Woman," *St. Xavier's Echo*, July 1892, p. 69.

43. "Woman as President, Negative; Woman as President, Affirmative"; *St. Xavier's Echo*, April 1893, pp. 32-33; "Woman as

President, Negative, Woman as President, Affirmative," *St. Xavier's Echo*, June 1893, pp. 52-53.

44. Catherine Donnelly, "Ruskin's Estimate of Woman," *The Young Eagle*, April 1905, p. 59, AOP.

45. Bertha Ball, "Views of Woman Suffrage," *The Labarium*, December 1912, p. 2.

46. Ibid., p. 6.

47. "Class Prophecy," *The Sesame*, St. Xavier's Yearbook, 1911.

48. The second half of Chapter V relies mostly on evidence from the alumnae of the academies of the Sacred Heart. Although the Sisters of Mercy, the Sinsinawa Dominicans and the B.V.M.'s had strong alumnae groups, these orders did not preserve much of their alumnae material. In addition, more information on Sacred Heart graduates exists because their economic and social position gave them greater opportunities to establish alumnae groups and magazines, engage in charity work, and become professional writers. The Society of the Sacred Heart also established convent schools throughout the United States and therefore had many more academy graduates than any other American religious order. However, my conclusions about convent school alumnae apply not only to Sacred Heart women but also to graduates of the other schools under study in this dissertation. Given the extraordinary similarity of the academic, social, and religious education provided at all the academies, attendance at any of these schools could hardly fail to produce girls with common values, aspirations, and ideals.

49. In addition to the sodalities attached to convent schools, parishes contained various female societies. For example, in two Chicago parishes where the B.V.M.'s maintained schools, there existed a number of sodalities. In 1910 St. Charles Borromeo reported in their Silver Jubilee Booklet that the Holy Maternity Sodality numbered 350 members while the Young Ladies Sodality had 292 members. Our Lady of Lourdes' 1916 celebration pamphlet of the church's dedication listed a Married Woman's Sodality, the Lourdes Women's Club and the Sanctuary Society of Our Lady of Lourdes, ABVM.

50. Children of Mary Minutes, 1875-1925, St. Louis, October 20, 1888, ARSCJ.

51. Ibid., January 30, 1900.

52. Journal of the Children of Mary, 1871-1920, Clifton, May 1871, ARSCJ.

53. Children of Mary Minutes, St. Louis, May 28, 1896 and February 1903, ARSCJ.

54. Journal of the Children of Mary, Clifton, October 7, 1898, ARSCJ.

55. Ibid., December 8, 1900.

56. Catholic women were noticeably absent from reform movements, especially suffrage. One of the few Catholics involved in this movement was Lucy Burns, a radical suffragette who served as vice-chairwoman of the National Women's Party. However, Burns's education sharply distinguished her from other Catholic women. She received a B.A. from Vassar in 1902 and did graduate work at Yale, the University of Berlin, and the University of Bonn. The Catholic clergy strongly criticized Catholic women like Lucy Burns who attended secular colleges and universities. The church believed that these institutions were especially dangerous to the faith and morals of young Catholic women. Numerous articles in the Catholic press and statements by bishops discussed the doubts and unbelief which plagued those students who attended a non-Catholic school. "Parents Who Send Their Daughters to Vassar," *American Ecclesiastical Review*, February 1899, p. 408; "Catholic Youth and Non-Catholic Colleges, Youth and the Catholic College," *The Review*, 7 January 1904, pp. 1-7 and "Concerning Convent Schools," *Ave Maria*, 11 April 1907, pp. 593-94.

57. Hasia Diner in *Erin's Daughters in America* attributes the anti-suffrage sentiment of Irish working-class women to the movement's middle-class bias and its anti-Catholic and anti-Irish sentiments. She notes that clerical opposition to the enfranchisement of women does not explain the small amount of Irish support given the enthusiastic participation of large numbers of Irish women in the labor movement, which the Church failed to support. The women who attended convent schools sharply differed in class, occupations, and attitude from the women described in Diner's book and they supported no liberal or progressive movement.

58. Mary V. Toomey, "Work and Aims of the Queen's Daughters," *Catholic World*, August 1898, pp. 610-21.

59. Children of Mary Role Book, St. Louis, 1875-1925, ARSCJ.

60. Mary Agnes Amberg, *Madonna Center* (Chicago: Loyola University Press, 1976).

61. Allen F. Davis and Mary Lynn McCree, eds., *Eighty Years at Hull House* (Chicago: Quadrangle Books, 1969).

62. "Report of Good Works," 1907-1908, St. Louis Children of Mary, ARSCJ.

63. Ultima Robinson Dooley, "To Our Second Mothers," *The Signet*, November 1923, p. 58.

64. Even Vassar College's conservative first president, John Raymond, believed that woman should have a choice not to marry. He told students that "if any love literature or art better than married life, that women should be free to choose." Quoted in Barbara Solomon, *In the Company of Educated Women*, p. 118.

65. "Alumnae Notes," *The Young Eagle*, February 1910, p. 83, AOP.

66. Famous writers who attended the academies of the Sacred Heart in the period under study included Agnes Repplier, Louise Imogen Guiney, Mary Catherine Crowley, Katherine E. Conway, Alice Worthington, Florence Gilmore, Mary Boyle O'Reilly, Elizabeth Boyle O'Reilly, Mary Elizabeth Blake, and Kate Chopin. All but the last two were single.

67. Alumnae notes from *The Young Eagle*, AOP.

68. Alumnae notes from *The Labarium* and *St. Xavier's Echo*.

69. Annette C. Washburne, M.D., "The Autobiography of a Medical Student," *The Signet*, October 1931; and Mary Agnes Amberg, "The Sacred Heart Girl in Chicago's Social Service," *The Signet*, October 1928.

70. A few notes on wayward alumnae appeared in the Student Register of the Academy of the Sacred Heart, Chicago and Lake Forest, 1858-1920. One student attending the academy from 1906 to 1908 "gave up her faith for a brilliant marriage to a titled Englishman." A later entry noted that she had divorced. Two sisters who went to the academy from 1907 to 1912 married Jewish men. A pupil attending the school during the years 1919 and 1920 divorced, took back her name and remarried. The Archives of the Academy of the Sacred Heart, Lake Forest.

71. George S. Stokes, *Agnes Repplier* (Philadelphia: University of Pennsylvania Press, 1949), p. 26.

72. Repplier, "Women Enthroned," in *Points of Friction* (Boston: Houghton Mifflin Co., 1920), p. 169.

73. Ibid., p. 202.

74. Repplier, "The Eternal Feminine," in *Varia*, (Boston: Houghton Mifflin Co., 1897), p. 20.

75. Ibid., p. 17.

76. Ibid., p. 28.

77. Repplier, "The Spinster," in *Compromises*, (Boston: Houghton Mifflin Co., 1904), p. 172.

78. Repplier, "Three Famous Old Maids," in *Essays in Miniature*, (Boston: Houghton Mifflin Co., 1892), p. 157.

79. Repplier, "The Spinster," p. 175.

80. Repplier, "Women Enthroned," p. 182.

81. Repplier, "The Spinster," p. 175.

82. Per Seyersted discusses the reaction to Chopin's novel in *Kate Chopin: A Critical Biography* (Baton Rouge: Louisiana State University Press, 1969), pp. 173-81.

83. Larzer Ziff, *The American 1890s* (Lincoln: University of Nebraska Press, 1966), p. 304.

84. Per Seyersted, p. 70.

85. Kate Chopin, "Wiser Than a God," in *The Complete Works of Kate Chopin*, 2 vols., ed. Per Seyersted (Baton Rouge: Louisiana State University Press) 1:48.

86. Other writers also saw a conflict between the woman's role and her artistic vocation in nineteenth-century America. For example, Rebecca Harding Davis *(Earthen Pitchers)*, Elizabeth Stuart Phelps *(The Story of Avis)*, Louisa May Alcott *(Little Women)*, and May Austin *(A Woman of Genius)*.

87. Chopin, "A Point at Issue," 1:50.

88. Chopin, "The Story of an Hour," 1:353-54.

89. Ibid., p. 354.

90. Chopin, *The Awakening*, in *The Complete Works*, 2:999. See n. 85 above.

91. Ibid., 2:888. Per Seyersted's interpretation of this novel influenced my description of it.

92. Chopin, "A Vocation and a Voice," in *The Complete Works*, 2:546.

93. Per Seyersted, p. 168.

94. Chopin, "The Storm," in *The Complete Works*, 2:595.

95. Ibid., p. 596.

96. Holy Picture Souvenir, 1916 Children of Mary Retreat, St. Louis, ARSCJ.

Conclusion

1. Sister Mary Isabel, Autograph Album of Johanna Morgan, Class of 1880, St. Xavier Academy, ASM.

Bibliography

Archival Sources

The National Archives of the Society of the Sacerd Heart in the United States (ARSCJ), St. Louis, Missouri. These archives hold materials on each mission of the Society in America. Those materials directly relevant to this study are the following:

a. St. Louis, City House: Student Register; Prospectuses; House Journals; Pupils' Account Books; Notes on Meetings of the Adult Children of Mary; List of Books in the Children of Mary Library; Children of Mary Rule Books; Children of Mary Report of Good Works; Annual Reports of the Children of Mary. Maryville: Journal of Sisters; Annual Distribution of Premiums; List of Subjects; Journal of the Boarding School; Notes on Janet Erskine Stuart's Conferences on Education; Student Account Books; Alumnae Year Book; Alumnae Directory; Student Newspapers; Plan of Studies.

b. Clifton: House Journals; Letters of the Superiors of the House; Register of Students; Minutes of the Children of Mary; Minutes of the Adult Children of Mary;

Minutes of the Angels; Pupils' Account Books; Surveillante Generalé's Memorial.

c. Chicago, Taylor Street: Vicariate tests; Reminiscences; House Journals; Instructions for the Administration of the School; Alumnae material; Memorials of the Visits of the Vicar.

d. St. Joseph, Missouri: House Journals; Memorials of the Visits of the Vicar; Student Register; Alumnae Yearbook.

e. *The Signet,* Alumnae magazine; Janet Erskine Stuart's Conferences.

Archives of the Academy of the Sacred Heart, Sheridan Road, Chicago: Subject of classes; School Journals; Student Register for the Society of the Sacred Heart Day School.

Archives of the Academy of the Sacred Heart, Lake Forest, Illinois: Student Register, Taylor Street, Chicago and Lake Forest.

Archives of the Sisters of Mercy of Chicago (ASM), Chicago, Illinois:

a. The Sisters: Rules and Constitutions; Custom Books; Chapter Books; Log Books; Novice Guide; Letters and Writings of the Sisters; Record of Entrants and Departures.

b. St. Xavier Academy: Courses of Study; Book Lists; *The St. Xavier Echo,* student newspaper; Examination Questions; Catalogues; Student Test Books; Alumnae Association material.

Archives of the Sisters of Charity of the Blessed Virgin Mary (ABVM), Dubuque, Iowa:

a. The Sisters: Rules and Constitutions; Diaries; List of Entrants and Departures; Book of Common Observance; Letters; Annals.

b. The Schools: Immaculate Conception Academy Catalogues; Mt. St. Joseph Academy Catalogues; St. Francis Academy Catalogues; *The Labarium,* Mt. St. Joseph Student newspaper; Clark College Alumnae File; Im-

maculate Conception Alumnae List; Mt. Carmel
Academy Alumnae List.

Archives of the Sinsinawa Dominicans (AOP), Sinsinawa,
Wisconsin:
  a. The Sisters: Rules and Constitutions; Annals; Notes
     and Diaries; Record of Entrants and Departures; Let-
     ters; Reminiscences.
  b. The Schools: St. Clara Academy Catalogues; Sacred
     Heart Academy Catalogues; *The Young Eagle*, St. Clara
     student publication; Reminiscences; Student Essays;
     Oral History Collection.

Archives of the University of Notre Dame, Notre Dame, Indiana.

Other Primary Sources

Ancient and Modern History. New York: William H. Sadlier,
1884.

Brothers of the Christian Schools. *Lessons in English.* New
York: William H. Sadlier, 1889.

Carroll, Mother Mary Teresa Austin. *Leaves from the Annals of
the Sisters of Mercy.* 4 vols. New York: P. O'Shea, 1881,
1883, 1888, 1895.

Chopin, Kate. *The Complete Works of Kate Chopin.* Edited by
Per Seyersted. 2 vols. Baton Rouge: Louisiana State University Press, 1969.

Complete Bible History. New York: D. & J. Sadlier & Co., 1891.

Coogan, B.V.M., Sister Mary St. Joan. "History of the Immaculate Conception Academy of Davenport, Iowa."
M.A. Thesis, Catholic University 1941.

Cook, Katherine M. *State Laws and Regulations Governing
Teachers' Certificates.* Washington: Government Printing
Office, 1921.

Enfant de Marie [pseud.]. "School Days at the Sacred Heart."
Putnam's Magazine, March 1870, pp. 275-86.

Excelsior Fourth Reader. New York: D. & J. Sadlier & Co., 1904.

The Fourth Progressive Reader. New York: P. O'Shea, 1871.

A Guide for the Religious Called the Sisters of Mercy. London: St. Anne's Press, 1888.

Lessons in English. New York: William H. Sadlier, 1893.

Mazzuchelli, Samuel, O.P. *Memoirs: Historical and Edifying of a Missionary Apostolic*. Translated by Sister Mary Benedicta Kennedy, O.P. Chicago: W. G. Hall Printing Co., 1915.

O'Brien, Mother Gabriel, R.S.M. *Reminiscences of Seventy Years, 1846-1916: Sisters of Mercy, St. Xavier's, Chicago*. Chicago: Fred J. Rengley, 1916.

Peacock, Virginia Tatmall. "The Sacred Heart Order: An Educational Factor in North America." *Donaghoe's Magazine*, February 1897, pp. 121-36.

Repplier, Agnes. *Americans and Others*. Boston: Houghton Mifflin Co., 1912.

――――. *Compromises*. Boston: Houghton Mifflin Co., 1904.

――――. *Essays in Miniature*. Boston: Houghton Mifflin Co., 1892.

――――. *In Our Convent Days*. Boston: Houghton Mifflin Co., 1905.

――――. *Points of Friction*. Boston: Houghton Mifflin Co., 1920.

――――. *Varia*. Boston: Houghton Mifflin Co., 1897.

Harriet Rose Collection 1833-1922. Chicago Historical Society.

Rule and Constitutions of the Religious Sisters of Mercy. Philadelphia: H. L. Kilner & Co., 1890.

Rule of the School and Plan of Studies of the Society of the Sacred Heart of Jesus. Translated by the Society of the Sacred Heart. Roehampton, England: The Society of the Sacred Heart, 1904.

The Rule of the Third Order of St. Dominic. New York: Sadlier & Co., 1860.

Sadlier, Mrs. James. *The Young Ladies' Reader.* New York: D. & J. Sadlier & Co., 1885.

Sadlier's Excelsior Compendium of Literature and Elocution. New York: William H. Sadlier, 1878.

Sadlier's Excelsior Fifth Reader. New York: William H. Sadlier, 1877.

Sadlier's History of the United States. New York: William H. Sadlier, 1879.

Sadlier's New Intermediate Reader. New York: William H. Sadlier's Sons, 1911.

St. Joseph's Convent, Mt. Carmel, Dubuque, 1833-1887. *In the Early Days: Pages from the Annals of the Sisters of Charity of the Blessed Virgin Mary.* St. Louis: B. Herder, 1912.

Shields, Thomas E. *The Education of Our Girls.* New York: Benziger Bros., 1907.

Sisters of Charity of the B.V.M., eds. *Woman: A Collection of Tributes to Woman.* Davenport, Iowa: Gorman & Son, 1893.

Stevens, Sister Charles Borromeo, O.S.D. [Carola Milanis]. *Golden Bells in Convent Towers.* Chicago: Lakeside Press, 1904.

_____ . *Little Essays for Friendly Readers.* Dubuque: M. S. Hardie Co., 1909.

Stuart, Janet Erskine, R.S.C.J. *The Education of Catholic Girls.* London: Longmans, Green & Co., 1911.

The United States Catholic Almanac or Laity's Directory. Baltimore: J. Myres, 1834. *The Metropolitan Catholic Almanac and Laity's Directory.* Baltimore: Fielding Lucas, 1838-1857. *American Catholic Almanac and List of Clergy.* New York: Ed. Dunigan Bros., 1858. *Metropolitan Catholic Almanac and Laity's Directory.* Baltimore: John Murphy & Son, 1859-1860. *Sadlier's Catholic Almanac and Ordo.* New York: D. & J. Sadlier, 1864-1894. *Hoffman's Catholic Directory.* Milwaukee: M. H. Wiltzins & Co., 1895-1899. *Catholic Directory, Almanac and Clergy List.* Milwaukee: M. H.

Wiltzins & Co., 1900-1911. *The Official Catholic Directory and Clergy List*. New York: P. J. Kennedy & Sons, 1912-1920.

Young Ladies Illustrated Reader. New York: The Catholic Publication Society, 1889.

Periodical Sources

American Ecclesiastical Review

America

American Catholic Quarterly Review

American Ecclesiastical Review

Ave Maria

The Bulletin

Catholic World

The Catholic Education Association Bulletin

The Catholic Educational Review

The Catholic Fortnightly Review

The Catholic Mind

The Catholic School and Home Magazine

The Catholic School Journal

The Dolphin

Fraser's Magazine (British)

History of Education Quarterly

Messenger of the Sacred Heart

Putnam's Magazine

Sacred Heart Review

Secondary Sources

Amberg, Mary Agnes. *Madonna Center.* Chicago: Loyola University Press, 1976.

Aubert, Roger. *The Church in a Secularized Society.* London: Darton, Longmans & Todd, 1978.

Augustine, Mother Flavia. "Cultural and Religious Effects of the Convent of the Sacred Heart of St. Joseph, Missouri, on Its Region During Its One Hundred Years of Existence." Master's thesis, Creighton University, 1952.

Barnard, H. C., ed. *Fénelon on Education.* Cambridge: University Press, 1966.

———. *Madame de Maintenon and Saint-Cyr.* London: A. & C. Black, 1934.

Bowler, Sister Mary Mariella. "A History of Catholic Colleges for Women in the United States of America." Ph.D. dissertation, Catholic University of America, 1933.

Brackett, Anna C., ed. *Woman and the Higher Education.* New York: Harper & Bros., 1893.

Brown, Judith C. *Immodest Acts.* New York: Oxford University Press, 1986.

Brown, Sister Mary Borromeo. *The History of the Sisters of Providence of St. Mary-of-the-Woods.* Vol. I. New York: Benziger Bros., 1949.

Burns, Rev. James A. *Catholic Education: A Study of Conditions.* New York: Longmans, Green & Co., 1917.

———. *The Catholic School System in the United States: Its Principles, Origins and Establishment.* New York: Benziger Bros., 1908.

———. *The Growth and Development of the Catholic School System in the United States.* New York: Benziger Bros., 1912.

——— and Kohlbrenner, Bernard J. *A History of Catholic Education in the United States.* New York: Benziger Bros., 1937.

Burstall, Sara A. *The Education of Girls in the United States.* London: Swan Sonnenschein & Co., 1894.

Butts, R. Freeman. *Public Education in the United States*. New York: Holt, Rinehart & Winston, 1978.

Cain, James R. *The Influence of the Cloister on the Apostolate of Congregations of Religious Women*. Rome: Pontifical University, 1965.

Callahan, Nelson, ed. *The Diary of Richard L. Burtsell, Priest of New York*. New York: Arno Press, 1978.

Callan, Louise, R.S.C.J. *Philippine Duchesne: Frontier Missionary of the Sacred Heart*. Maryland: Newman Press, 1957.

_____. *The Society of the Sacred Heart in North America*. London: Longmans, Green & Co., 1937.

Callan, Sister Mary Anna Rose, B.V.M. "The Sisters of Charity of the B.V.M. and their Schools in Chicago, 1867-1940." Master's thesis, Loyola University of Chicago, 1941.

Carr, Elizabeth Worland. "American Catholic Women and the Church to 1920." Ph.D. dissertation, St. Louis University, 1982.

Conroy, Joseph P., S.J. *Arnold Damen, S.J.* New York: Benziger Bros., 1930.

Converse, Florence. *Wellesley College*. Wellesley, Massachusetts: Hathaway House Bookshop, 1939.

Convey, Sister Mary Fidelis. "Mother Agatha O'Brien and the Pioneers." Master's thesis, Loyola University of Chicago, 1929.

Conway, Jill. "Perspectives on the History of Women's Education in the United States." *History of Education Quarterly* 14 (Spring 1974): 1-12.

Coogan, M. Jane, B.V.M. *Mary Frances Clarke: Foundress*. Dubuque: Mount Carmel Press, 1977.

_____. *The Price of Our Heritage*. 2 vols. Dubuque: Mount Carmel Press, 1978.

Cott, Nancy F. *The Bonds of Womanhood*. New Haven: Yale University Press, 1977.

_____ and Pleck, Elizabeth, eds. *A Heritage of Her Own*. New York: Simon & Schuster, 1979.

Cremin, Lawrence. *American Education: The National Experience, 1783-1876*. New York: Harper & Row, 1980.

——. *The Transformation of the Schools: Progressivism in American Education, 1876-1957*. New York: Knopf, 1961.

——. *Traditions of American Education*. New York: Basic Books, 1977.

Cross, Barbara, ed. *The Educated Woman in America: Selected Writings of Catherine Beecher, Margaret Fuller, and M. Carey Thomas*. New York: Teachers' College Press, 1965.

Crump, C. G. and E. F. Jacobs. *The Legacy of the Middle Ages*. Oxford: Clarendon Press, 1926.

Deferrari, Roy J., ed. *Vital Problems of Catholic Education in the United States*. Washington, D.C.: Catholic University of America Press, 1939.

Degnan, Sister Bertrand. *Mercy Unto Thousands: Life of Mother Mary Catherine McAuley*. Maryland: Newman Press, 1957.

Dehey, Elinor. *Religious Orders of Women in the United States*. Indiana: W. B. Conkey, 1930.

Diner, Hasia R. *Erin's Daughters in America: Irish Immigrant Women in the Nineteenth Century*. Baltimore: The Johns Hopkins University Press, 1983.

Dobkin, Marjorie Housepian, ed. *The Making of a Feminist: Early Journals and Letters of M. Carey Thomas*. Ohio: Kent State University Press, 1979.

Dolan, Jay. *Catholic Revivalism: The American Experience, 1830-1900*. Notre Dame: University of Notre Dame Press, 1978.

Douglas, Ann. *The Feminization of American Culture*. New York: Alfred A. Knopf, 1977.

Doyle, Sister Margaret Mary. "The Curriculum of the Catholic Woman's College." Ph.D. dissertation, University of Notre Dame, 1932.

Elson, Ruth M. *Guardians of Tradition: American Schoolbooks of the Nineteenth Century*. Lincoln: University of Nebraska Press, 1964.

Evans, Mary Ellen. *The Spirit is Mercy: The Story of the Sisters of Mercy in the Archdiocese of Cincinnati, 1858-1958*. Maryland: Newman Press, 1959.

Ewens, Mary. *The Role of the Nun in Nineteenth-Century America*. New York: Arno Press, 1978.

Francis, Sister Catherine, S.S.J. "The Convent School of French Origin in the United States, 1727-1843." Ph.D. dissertation, University of Pennsylvania, 1936.

Frankfort, Roberta. *Collegiate Women: Domesticity and Career in Turn-of-the-Century America*. New York: New York University Press, 1977.

Galvin, Sister Mary Camillus. *From Acorn to Oak: A Study of Presentation Foundations, 1771-1968*. Fargo, North Dakota: Presentation Sisters, 1968.

Garraghan, Gilbert, S.J. *The Jesuits of the Middle United States*. 3 vols. New York: America Press, 1938.

Garvey, Mary, R.S.C.J. *Mary Aloysia Hardy*. New York: Longmans, Green & Co., 1925.

Gilligan, Sister Mary Clare, O.P. "A History of Edgewood." Master's thesis, De Paul University, 1948.

Goodsell, Willystine. *The Education of Women*. New York: The Macmillan Co., 1923.

Gordon, Lynne D. "Women With Missions: Varieties of College Life in the Progressive Era." Ph.D. dissertation, the University of Chicago, 1980.

Graves, Frank Pierrepont. *A History of Education during the Middle Ages and the Transition to Modern Times*. New York: Macmillan Co., 1910.

Green, Elizabeth A. *Mary Lyon and Mount Holyoke*. New Hampshire: University Press of New England, 1979.

Hagan, John Raphael. "The Diocesan Teachers College." Ph.D. dissertation, Catholic University, 1932.

Healy, Kathleen. *Frances Warde: American Founder of the Sisters of Mercy*. New York: Seabury Press, 1973.

Hennesey, James, S.J. *American Catholicism*. New York: Oxford University Press, 1981.

Hickey, Ann Ewing. *Women of the Senatoreal Aristocracy of Late Rome as Christian Monastics*. Ann Arbor: U.M.I. Research Press, 1986.

Holland, Dorothy Garesché. "Maryville—The First One Hundred Years." *The Bulletin* 29 (April 1973):145-162.

Hunter, Jane. *The Gospel of Gentility*. New Haven: Yale University Press, 1984.

James, Janet Wilson, ed. *Women in American Religion*. Philadelphia: University of Pennsylvania Press, 1980.

Johnson, Paul. *History of Christianity*. New York: Atheneum, 1977.

Kett, Joseph F. *Rites of Passage*. New York: Basic Books, 1977.

Klein, Christa Ressmeyer. "The Jesuits and Catholic Boyhood in Nineteenth-Century New York City: A Study of St. John's College and the College of St. Francis Xavier." Ph.D. dissertation, University of Pennsylvania, 1976.

Krug, Edward. *The Shaping of the American High School*. New York: Harper & Row, 1964.

Labalme, Patricia, ed. *Beyond Their Sex: Learned Women of the European Past*. New York: New York University Press, 1980.

Life and Life-Work of Mother Theodore Guerin. New York: Benziger Bros., 1904.

Lord, Daniel A., S.J. *Our Nuns*. New York: Benziger Bros., 1924.

Louise, Sister Helen. *Sister Julia*. New York: Benziger Bros., 1928.

Lucas, Angela M. *Women in the Middle Ages*, New York: St. Martin's Press, 1983.

McCarthy, Mary. *Memories of a Catholic Girlhood*. New York: Harcourt, Brace & Co., 1946.

McCarty, Sister Mary Eva, O.P. *The Sinsinawa Dominicans: Outlines of Twentieth Century Development, 1901-1949*. Dubuque: Hoermann Press, 1952.

McDonnell, Colleen. *The Christian Home in Victorian America, 1840-1900*. Bloomington: Indiana University Press, 1986.

McGreal, Sister Mary Nona, O.P. "The Role of the Teaching Sisterhood in American Education." Ph.D. dissertation, Catholic University of America, 1951.

McHale, Sister Mary Jerome. *On the Wing: The Story of the Pittsburgh Sisters of Mercy, 1843-1968*. New York: Seabury Press, 1980.

Melville, Annabelle M. *Elizabeth Bayley Seton, 1774-1821*. New York: Charles Scribner's Sons, 1951.

Messbarger, Paul R. *Fiction With A Parochial Purpose*. Notre Dame: University of Notre Dame Press, 1971.

Misner, Barbara. "A Comparative Social Study of the Members and Apostolates of the First Eight Permanent Communities of Women Religious Within the Original Boundaries of the United States, 1790-1850." Ph.D. dissertation, Catholic University of America, 1981.

Monahan, Maud, R.S.C.J. *Life and Letters of Janet Erskine Stuart*. London: Longmans, Green & Co., 1922.

Monica, Sister Mary. *Angela Merici and Her Teaching Idea, 1474-1540*. London: Longmans, Green & Co., 1927.

Montay, Sister Mary Innocenta. "The History of Catholic Secondary Education in the Archdiocese of Chicago." Ph.D. dissertation, Catholic University of America, 1952.

Moran, Jo Ann Hoeppner. *The Growth of English Schools 1340-1548*. New Jersey: Princeton University Press, 1985.

Mrozek, Donald J. *Sport and American Mentality 1880-1910*. Knoxville: University of Tennessee Press, 1983.

Murphy, Mother Mary Benedict, R.S.H.M. "Pioneer Roman Catholic Girls Academies: Their Growth, Character and Contribution to American Education." Ph.D. dissertation, Columbia University, 1958.

Neumann, Sister Mary Ignatia, R.S.M., ed. *Letters of Catherine McAuley*. Baltimore: Helicon Press, 1969.

Noonan, John T. Jr. *Contraception: A History of Its Treatment by the Catholic Theologians and Canonists*. Cambridge: Harvard University Press, 1965.

Nugent, Sister Helen Louise. *Sister Louise: Josephine van der Schrieck, 1813-1886, American Foundress of the Sisters of Notre Dame de Namur.* New York: Benziger Bros., 1931.

O'Connor, Mother Mary Isadore. *Life of Mary Monholland: One of the Pioneer Sisters of the Order of Mercy in the West.* Chicago: J. S. Hyland & Co., 1894.

O'Connor, Mother Mary Margarita. *That Incomparable Woman.* Montreal: Palm Publishers, 1962.

O'Connor, Sister Mary Paschala, O.P. *Five Decades: History of the Congregation of the Most Holy Rosary, Sinsinawa, Wisconsin, 1849-1899.* Sinsinawa, Wisconsin: Sinsinawa Press, 1954.

O'Leary, Mary. *Education with a Tradition.* New York: Longmans, Green, 1936.

O'Reilly, Bernard. *The Mirror of True Womanhood and True Men As We Need Them.* New York: P. J. Kenedy, 1887.

Pope, Christie. "Preparation for Pedestals: North Carolina Antebellum Female Seminaries." Ph.D. dissertation, University of Chicago, 1977.

Power, Eileen. *Medieval English Nunneries.* Cambridge: Cambridge University Press, 1922; reprint edition, New York: Bilbo & Tanner, 1964.

_____. *Medieval Women.* Edited by M. M. Postan. Cambridge: Cambridge University Press, 1975.

Quinlan, Mary C., R.S.C.J. *Mabel Digby—Janet Erskine Stuart.* n.p., Sacred Heart Higher Education Association, 1982.

Rankin, Daniel. "Kate Chopin and Her Creole Stories." Ph.D. dissertation, University of Pennsylvania, 1932.

Rudolf, Frederick. *Curriculum: A History of the American Undergraduate Course of Study Since 1636.* San Francisco: Jossey-Bass, 1977.

Ruether, Rosemary and McLaughlin, Eleanor. *Women of Spirit: Female Leadership in the Jewish and Christian Tradition.* New York: Simon & Schuster, 1979.

Sand, George. *My Convent Life*. Trans. Maria Ellery McKay. Boston: Roberts, 1893; reprint ed., Chicago: Academy Press, 1978.

Sanders, James W. *The Education of an Urban Minority*. New York: Oxford University Press, 1977.

Savage, Sister Mary Lucida. *The Congregation of St. Joseph of Carondelet*. St. Louis: B. Herder, 1923.

Savage, Roland, S.J. *Catherine McAuley*. Dublin: M. H. Gill & Son, 1949.

A School Sister of Notre Dame. *Mother Caroline and the School Sisters of Notre Dame in North America*. Vol. 1. St. Louis: Woodward & Tiernan, 1928.

Scott, Ann Firor. "The Ever Widening Circle: The Diffusion of Feminist Values from the Troy Female Seminary, 1822-1872." *History of Education Quarterly* 19 (Spring 1979):3-25.

Seelye, L. Clark. *The Early History of Smith College, 1871-1910*. Boston: Houghton Mifflin Co., 1923.

Seyersted, Per. *Kate Chopin: A Critical Biography*. Baton Rouge: Louisiana State University Press, 1969.

_____ and E. Toth, eds. *A Kate Chopin Miscellany*. Natchitoches: Northwestern State University Press, 1979.

Shanabruch, Charles. *Chicago's Catholics: The Evolution of an American Identity*. Notre Dame: Notre Dame Press, 1981.

Sklar, Kathryn Kish. *Catherine Beecher: A Study in American Domesticity*. New Haven: Yale University Press, 1973.

Smith, Bonnie G. *Ladies of the Leisure Class: The Bourgeoises of Northern France in the Nineteenth Century*. Princeton: Princeton University Press, 1981.

Smith, Page. *Daughters of the Promised Land*. Boston: Little, Brown & Co., 1970.

Smith-Rosenberg, Carroll. "The Female World of Love and Ritual: Relations Between Women in Nineteenth-Century America." *Signs* 1 (Autumn 1975):1-29.

Solomon, Barbara M. *In the Company of Educated Women: A History of Women and Higher Education in America.* Conn.: Yale University Press, 1985.

Spears, Betty and Richard Swansen. *History of Sport and Physical Activity in the United States,* 2d. ed, Dubuque: Wm. C. Brown Co., 1983.

Stokes, George Stuart. *Agnes Repplier.* Philadelphia: University of Pennsylvania Press, 1949.

Stout, John Elbert. *The Development of High-School Curriculum in the North Central States from 1860 to 1890.* Chicago: University of Chicago Press, 1921.

Synon, Mary. *Mother Emily of Sinsinawa.* Milwaukee: Bruce Publishing Co., 1955.

Talbot, Marion. *The Education of Women.* Chicago: The University of Chicago Press, 1910.

Taves, Ann. *The Household of Faith:* Roman Catholic Devotions in Mid-Nineteenth Century America. Indiana: University of Notre Dame Press, 1986.

Taylor, James Monroe and Haight, Elizabeth Hazelton. *Vassar.* New York: Oxford University Press, 1915.

Thomas, Sister Mary Evangeline. *Footsteps on the Frontier: History of the Sisters of St. Joseph of Concordia, Kansas.* Maryland: Newman Press, 1948.

Tyack, David B. *The One Best System: A History of Urban Education.* Cambridge: Harvard University Press, 1974.

Walsh, Timothy. "Catholic Education in Chicago and Milwaukee, 1840-1890." Ph.D. dissertation, Northwestern University, 1976.

Walsh, T. J. *Nano Nagle and the Presentation Sisters.* Dublin: M. H. Gill & Son, 1959.

Warner, Marina. *Alone of All Her Sex.* New York: Alfred A. Knopf, 1976.

Watson, Foster, ed. *Vives and the Renascence Education of Women.* London: Edward Arnold, 1912.

Welter, Barbara. *Dimity Convictions: The American Woman in the Nineteenth Century.* Athens, Ohio: Ohio University Press, 1976.

Wemple, Suzanne F. *Women in Frankish Society: Marriage and the Cloister, 500 to 900.* Philadelphia: University of Pennsylvania Press, 1981.

White, Antonia. *Frost in May.* New York: Dial Press, 1933.

Williams, Margaret, R.S.C.J. *Saint Madeleine Sophie: Her Life and Letters.* New York: Herder & Herder, 1965.

———. *The Society of the Sacred Heart: History of a Spirit, 1800-1975.* London: Darton, Longman & Todd, 1978.

Woodward, William. *Studies in Education During the Age of the Renaissance, 1400-1600.* New York: Russell & Russell, 1965.

Woody, Thomas. *A History of Women's Education in the United States.* 2 vols. New York: The Science Press, 1929.

Index

charity, 118, 120
chastity, 19, 43, 93, 115
Chicago, nuns in, 16, 29, 31
childbirth, 102, 106
Children of Mary (Chicago), 119, 120
Children of Mary (St. Louis), 117-119, 120
Chopin, Kate (nee O'Flaherty), 125, 128-32
Cincinnati, nuns in, 16
City House (St. Louis), 46, 47
Clarke, Mary Frances, 30, 31, 37, 39
communities, see religious communities, female
convents, see religious communities, female
convent schools:
  criticism of, 60ff., 124ff., 137
  curriculum of, 9, 34-35, 45, 48, 76
  genesis of, 15, 35
  in the Midwest, 16, 24ff., 46, 51
  non-Catholic students, 87ff
  objectives of, 35ff., 45, 46
  for the underprivileged, 27
  for the upper class, 24, 26, 48, 60, 76
  of the Ursulines, 4, 7
  See also Sinsinawa Dominicans, Sisters of Charity, Sisters of Mercy, Sisters of Notre Dame, Society of the Sacred Heart
conversion, 10
Conway, Katherine, 107
Coughlin, Mother Samuel, 102
Creighton University, 41
curriculum, see convent schools, curriculum of

Damen, Rev. Arnold, 31
Dames of Saint-Louis, The, 7

Davenport, Iowa, convent school in, 16, 46
De Paul University (Chicago), 41
Digby, Mabel, 60
Discalced Carmelite Nuns, 14
discipline, 65-66
domestic science, 104-5
Dominican Fathers, 32
Donaghoe, Terence, 30, 32, 37
DuBourg, Bishop Louis, 25
Dubuque, Iowa, nuns in, 16, 30, 46
Duchesne, Philippine, 25-26

Edgeworth, Maria, 127
education, female:
  in America, 7, 11, 13
  Christian tradition of, 1
  Church of Rome's attitude toward, 5, 14, 25, 31
  in England, 5
  under female religious orders, 4, 7-9, 36, 39, 41-42, 61
  in France, (also Gaul), 4, 7
  in Germany, 2
  in Ireland, 30
  in Italy, 4
  Jesuit influence on, 5, 34, 40
  monastic, 2
  non-Catholic, 3, 36, 41
  reformers, 10
  in Spain, 3-4
  See also convent schools, religious communities, female
education, Jesuit, 5
education, male, 3
education, during Middle Ages, 1-3
Education of Girls, The, 6
Edwards, Rhoda Walker, 72
Egan, Maurice Francis, 40, 61
Elizabeth of Schonau, 3
English, study of, 52-54
Erasmus, 4

examinations, 57-58
expectations, 101
expulsion, 66, 73

fees, 41, 46-47
feast days, 64, 80-81, 83
Fénelon, Archbishop François, 6
fine arts, study of, 58
French, study of, 5, 9, 56

games, 67
Garrigan, Archbishop P. J., 110
German, study of, 47, 56
Gibbons, James Cardinal, 108
Gleason, Caroline, 122, 123
Glennon, Archbishop John, 74, 109
Gonzaga, Aloysius, 94
Granger, Sister Mary Genevieve, 102
Grant, Zilpah, 10
Greek, study of, 56, 104
Guardian Angels Sunday School (Chicago), 119, 120
Guiney, Louise Imogen, 71, 75, 91

Harrington, Ethel, 122
Hartford Female Seminary, (Conn.), 10
Herlinda and Renilda of Eyck, 2
Hildegarde of Bingen, 3
history, study of, 40, 50, 54-55, 91
holy days, 81
Holy Family parish (Chicago), 31
homemakers, see wife
Hrowsitha, 2
Hudson, Daniel, 27
Hull-House (Chicago), 119
humility, 62
husbands, 106

Ignatius, St., 91
Illinois General Hospital (Mercy Hospital), 29
Immaculate Conception Academy (Iowa), 46, 48, 69
Ipswich Female Seminary, 10
Ireland, Bishop John, 108
Isabella, Mother, 102

Jerome, St., 1
Jesuits, Society of, 26
Jewish students, 88
Joseph Emerson's Ladies Seminary (Conn.), 10

Keane, Archbishop John J., 110
Kelly, Eliza, 30
Kenwood Academy of the Sacred Heart, 39
Kildare Place Schools, 36
Kildare Place Society, 35

Labarium, The, 114
language, study of, 9, 56
Latin, study of, 5, 56
literacy, 52
literature, study of, 40, 52, 91ff.
Longworth, Alice Roosevelt, 70
Loras, Bishop Matthew (Dubuque), 30
Loyola University (Chicago), 41
Lyon, Mary, 10

McAuley, Catherine, 27-28, 35
McGlynn, Edward, 108
McGlynn, Stephen, 26
McNicholas, Archbishop John T., 110
McNulty, Mary, 32
McQuaid, Bernard, 108

Madonna Center (Chicago), 123
Magnus, Albertus, 35

Quarter, Bishop William, 29
Queen's Daughters (St. Louis), 118

Ratio Studiorum, 34
recreation, 45, 65, 66-67
Reglements (Ursulines), 4
religion, study of, 5, 8, 10, 48, 49
religious communities, female:
  age of entrants, 23, 46, 48
  American, 13-24, 31
  Canadian, 13
  chapter of faults, 21
  community, idea of, 21-22, 41
  constitutions of, 20
  contributions of, 15, 98-99
  difficulties, personality, 21
  European missionaries, 13
  friendships forbidden, 20, 74
  growth of, 13ff.
  locations in the Midwest, 16
  novices, 18, 39
  objectives, 23ff., 34, 37, 43, 48
  penances, 19, 21
  postulants, 18
  rules, 20
  schedules, 5
  vows, 18
  See also nuns, Sinsiniwa
    Dominicans, Sisters of
    Charity, Sisters of Mercy,
    Sisters of Notre Dame, and
    Society of the Sacred Heart
religious observances, 79ff.
religious orders, see religious
  communities, female
Renaissance, 3ff.
Repplier, Agnes, 67, 68, 74, 81,
  85, 125-28
retreats, 19, 83-85
Roosevelt, Theodore, 70
Routtan, Mary, 32
Rule of St. Augustine, 19
rules of convent schools, 45, 72-
  73

Sacred Heart academies, 24-26,
  46, 51, 58, 59, 60, 64-66, 67, 88
  See also Academy of the
    Sacred Heart (Chicago),
    (Clifton), (Madison),
    Maryville (St. Louis), and
    City House (St. Louis)
St. Clara Academy (Sinsinawa
  and Benton, Wis.), 33, 46, 47,
  50, 51, 53, 55, 57, 58, 61, 64,
  66, 67, 69, 70, 73, 80, 89, 95,
  96, 97, 104, 109, 110
Saint-Cyr School, 6
St. Joseph Academy (Dubuque,
  Ia.), 46
St. Louis, nuns in, 16
St. Louis University, 41
St. Omer, 5
St. Xavier Academy (Chicago),
  46, 47, 50, 51, 53, 55, 58, 63,
  64, 65, 69, 70, 75, 87, 88, 95,
  112, 114, 122, 135
St. Xavier's Echo, 70, 71
salvation, 44
Sand, George, 43
San Vito, Joseph, 33
Sarah Pierce's Academy
  (Litchfield), 9
schedules (samples), 5, 8, 63-64,
  84
schools, see convent schools,
  Kildare Place Schools, parish
  schools, and public schools
science, study of, 40, 57
Scully, Thomas, 108
Seeyle, L. Clark (Smith College),
  111
Shields, Dr. Thomas, 40
silence, 8, 20, 65, 84
single women, 112ff., 121-123,
  132
Sinsinawa College (Wisc.), 110
Sinsinawa Dominicans, 20, 23,
  24, 31-33, 38, 40, 45, 58
Sinsinawa Mound, Wisc., 31, 33

217